THE HOLY SPIRIT

Scripture Union, 207–209 Queensway, Bletchley, MK2 2EB, England

Email: info@scriptureunion.org.uk
Web site: www.scriptureunion.org.uk

First published 1984, fully revised edition 2001

ISBN 1 85999 527 6

British Library Cataloguing-in-Publication Data.
A catalogue record of this book is available from the British Library.

Printed and bound in Great Britain by Creative Print and Design (Wales)
Ebbw Vale.

*Scripture Union is an international Christian charity working with churches in more
than 130 countries providing resources to bring the good news about Jesus Christ to
children, young people and families – and to encourage them to develop spiritually
through the Bible and prayer.*

*As well as our network of volunteers, staff and associates who run holidays, church-
based events and school Christian groups, we produce a wide range of publications and
support those who use our resources through training programmes.*

THE HOLY SPIRIT

TRANSFORMING US AND OUR WORLD

CLIVE CALVER

To Graham Kendrick

because without his friendship and support in the early years, some of this book could never have been written, and without it now, some of the rest would not be taking place.

Contents

Foreword

When I first preached at a United Methodist Church in Pensacola, Florida, I was fascinated to discover that it was a church with quite a traditional form of worship. There was a choir, robed altar boys and a fairly liturgical format. It was a church which, I soon discovered, had been recently touched by the powerful movement of the Holy Spirit in the same city. When I announced the first hymn and people stood to sing, the sense of the Holy Spirit was such that it was almost tangible. The reality of his presence was such that I could hardly stand. By the second verse, four people were kneeling at the altar rail in floods of tears, wanting to confess their sins and to get right with God.

By the time I was scheduled to preach, the altar rail was full, and the prayer team was at work among them. I turned to the pastor and asked if I should still speak! He urged me to do so, and as I continued yet more of the congregation came forward in repentance. While there are many aspects of such a 'revival' that I personally struggle with, and certain phenomena which bother me, I am left with one overwhelming response: if the Holy Spirit can move in renewing a fairly traditional United Methodist Church in suburban Florida, he can do it anywhere!

I came back from Pensacola with the personal feeling that I had sanitised the Holy Spirit and made him too safe! I returned with an urgent sense that the form of Christianity to be found in many of our churches needs the refreshing power of the Holy Spirit to shake us up and to remind us whose church it really is!

Clive Calver's book is an apposite and powerful challenge to seek for the Holy Spirit! There was certainly nothing safe about that first Pentecost described in the Acts of the Apostles! Luke described his arrival as like the 'blowing of a violent wind' which filled the whole house! Large fiery flames rushed through the house, divided, and rested on the individual disciples. They began to talk in strange languages! Scary stuff!

But why would God send a fresh anointing of the Holy Spirit upon his Church? In John 20: 21,22 Jesus tells his disciples that, as the Father has sent him ... so he is sending them! Immediately he breathes on them and tells them to receive the Holy Spirit. He's giving them power to fulfil the Great Commission!

Clive Calver helps us to understand that God doesn't send the Spirit to give us a warm glow inside or to get us dancing in the aisles! No. This book makes it clear that he sends him for mission. He sends him to help us to live. He sends him that we might witness. He sends him to give us gifts.

Clive's book comes at an important moment in the church history, for there are great dangers ahead. On the one side, there are those who question any kind of 'experience of the Holy Spirit' as relevant in the church today. On the other, there are those who seem so preoccupied with the work of the Holy Spirit' that they have no understanding of why he was given to us. They haven't done their biblical homework and are in danger of falling into serious error.

This book is reminiscent of John Wesley's teaching. His theology respected the authority of the Bible. He opposed the domination of reason which his Anglican contemporaries so appreciated, and defied the reliance on 'feelings' which was strongly advocated by revivalists. Wesley chose a middle way: an awesome respect for the Bible, but interpreted in the light of reason, church tradition and personal experience. His evangelistic fervour and his advocacy of 'the strangely warmed heart' challenged the cold deism of the established church. But at the same time he carefully protected his followers from the fanaticism which England had seen in the previous century.

In the same tradition, Clive Calver, one of the most influential church leaders of our time, maintains this vital sense of balance. His carefully weighed biblical appraisal of the work of the Holy Spirit is an important reminder that our experience must always be rooted in a solid understanding of what the Bible teaches. I believe that there will be many more waves of Holy Spirit renewal over the coming years, each one calling us to move beyond the familiar trappings of our comfortable Christianity and to complete the work that God has called us to do. Read Clive's book, and be prepared to receive the Holy Spirit in a new way yourself!

Rob Frost

Introduction

No book can ever be a completely solo project. Many people are involved at various stages and they should all receive their fair share of the blame! To complicate the situation further, many years have passed between the first and second editions. So my grateful thanks go to all who feature in these pages or who have contributed towards their production.

I do want to thank Scripture Union for its original invitation to contribute to a series of this nature. Particular thanks go to John Grayston, well-remembered as a 'demon' fast bowler from college days, whose contribution far exceeded his function as publishing editor, and to Andrew Clark, at whose insistence this revision was produced.

Writing the seminar notes for *Spring Harvest* during the closing months of 1990 provided a further opportunity to address this topic, and I would like to thank Peter Meadows, Alan Johnson, Steve Gaukroger, Martyn Eden, Ernest Lucas, Stanley Davies, Maggie Harding and especially Steve Chilcraft for their advice and assistance in that project. I also want to express my deep appreciation to all who have contributed through proof-reading and correcting this manuscript in terms of both style and content. Thanks are also due to the Evangelical Alliance for releasing me from time commitments and to Clive and Cindy Rolf for the loan of their home on the Isle of Wight, where much of this book was first written. Thanks go also to the Board of World Relief and to my colleagues for offering their support in allowing me the time and opportunity to complete four additional chapters as well as the substantial rewriting of the others.

Finally, I thank all my family and friends who are really a part of this book and the many who have provided inspiration and support over the years. I thank *you* for being prepared to read and share a dream and a prayer that God, by his Spirit, might keep us moving on with him into all that the future holds for us. For he has only made a beginning with each one of us, and by his grace, there will be still many chapters left to write.

Clive Calver
Baltimore
January 2001

Chapter 1

Missing pieces – missing person

Rhoda sits alone each day in the dust and the dirt of the streets of Lilongwe, the capital city of the East African country of Malawi. The reason Rhoda has to resort to her daily practice of begging is that she is blind and no employer would be prepared to adapt a job to suit her skills. So she is a beggar, and each day is occupied with just seeking to obtain enough money to eke out a frugal existence for herself and her mentally defective husband. His problems make it impossible for him to work, and consequently they have to be satisfied with living together in the unfurnished hovel which Rhoda calls 'home'.

Rhoda is a Christian. She is one of that worldwide family which will inhabit eternity with all those who, like her, love Jesus. As she sits there, sensing rather than seeing the people passing her by, Rhoda has every human reason for feeling resentful about the way that her life has turned out, for she nurses a small baby. This tiny squawking bundle of fragile humanity is not her own child but her granddaughter. Rhoda's daughter died of AIDS when the child was only a few days old. Now the blind grandmother is the only one left to care for the baby, and the child is almost certainly infected with the HIV virus transmitted from the mother.

On the morning my wife Ruth met Rhoda, this poor blind lady had just discovered that her water jar had been stolen from her side. It had been her only earthly possession.

In her inimitably straightforward style, Ruth asked a profound and significant question.

'Do you have any message you'd like me to take back from Africa to your brothers and sisters in the West?'

'Yes there is something I would like you to tell them,' came the instant reply. 'I want you to pass along the message that Rhoda is doing well and that all is fine for me here. Please say to my brothers and sisters that I have everything I could need, because I have Jesus.'

You and I may both want to marvel at the simple faith of this saint of God. We may wonder how it is that someone who possesses so little materially can have so much spiritually. We may question how it could be that someone who has been deprived of so much by the circumstances of life can somehow cling so tenaciously to the conviction that she is truly loved by God. We may well want to ask how she can be so positive in the face of such adversity. We may want to know what it is that has made her so convinced of the reality of the Lord's presence with her.

The answer is so simple and straightforward. The only credible explanation is that such faith is supernatural in origin. This can only be accounted for by the work of the Holy Spirit. It would certainly take the provision of divine strength and enabling for Rhoda to exhibit such supreme faith and confidence in the presence and power of Jesus working in her life.

The consistent demonstration of such dramatic qualities can originate only in the Holy Spirit himself. He has been called 'the author of every positive revolution in the history of the Church', 'Satan's unsolved problem' and 'God's secret weapon, bringing explosive life to his people'.

All of these descriptions may be perfectly accurate, but the sad truth is that during long periods of Christian history, the Holy Spirit has more often been regarded as the silent partner, the forgotten member of the Trinity. Too often he has received little or no acknowledgement. At times, he appears to have been almost subconsciously excluded from the Godhead.

This is a strange and unsatisfactory verdict on the Person who, within the Triune Godhead, communicates the love and presence of God. This is no mere external communication, for the Holy Spirit actually takes up residence within the lives of those of us who have surrendered ourselves to the forgiveness and saving love brought to us by Jesus Christ. In the final analysis, the Holy Spirit is no less than the very presence of the living God making his home in the life of the believer.

The problem boils down to the fact that Christians generally find it easier to understand and relate to God the Father and God the Son but much harder to grasp hold of the concept of God the Holy Spirit. While we find it relatively easy to wrap our minds around a Father who creates or a Son who walks in history, the notion of an apparently indefinable entity that comes from God to live within his people is another matter entirely. Yet he is actually the Person of the Godhead who takes up residence within our lives, and because he cannot be separated from the Father and the Son, brings them along, too!

The story is told of a clergyman's regular weekly visit to the local junior school. The children knew what to expect for each had been allocated a portion of the catechism to recite. One after the other, they proceeded until a silence interrupted the flow where the words 'I believe in the Holy Spirit' should have come. Eventually one child offered the explanation, 'Sorry, sir, the boy who believes in the Holy Spirit isn't here this morning!'

Sometimes we seem content to act in similar fashion. Tragically, our struggle to understand the nature and character of the Holy Spirit has often resulted in our unconsciously but effectively deleting him from the Trinity. This is sad because Christians have never accepted the picture of a God 'out there', some impersonal cosmic force dictating instructions to this minor planet, or even a God who is content merely to reveal himself through the pages of a book he has written. Nor have they accepted the image of a deity who interferes from time to time, making an occasional brief excursion into time and space, only to retreat quickly to a safe distance from where he can observe current developments in peace and quiet. No Christian can conceive of God as one who demands belief and faith while hiding in a corner of the universe, determined to remain unknown and unknowable. The wonder of the Christian gospel is that there is one God, the creator and ruler of heaven and earth – and he has no intention of keeping his distance!

That is why God walked and talked with Adam in the Garden of Eden (Gen 3:8,9).

That is why God took Israel to be his people in a specially agreed relationship (Deut 4:32–35).

That is why God spoke to his people through his servants the prophets and continued to send them even though they were rejected one after another (Ezek 2:1–7).

That is why God sent John the Baptist to prepare his people for the imminent birth on planet earth of his only begotten son, Jesus Christ (John 1:7).

That is why Jesus came, fully God and fully man, born in a cattle trough in a dirty Bethlehem stable (Luke 2:7).

That is why Jesus revealed his Father's love, fulfilling his mission by dying on a real cross at the hands of real men on a Jerusalem rubbish dump (Luke 23:33), breaking the power of sin and death.

There is something so wonderful in the way that God wanted to become intimately involved with people. Folk religions are full of stories about an arbitrary, capricious, transcendent being, a 'god' who was momentarily involved in the real world only to withdraw swiftly in disgust. Jesus was totally different. He portrayed the love of his Father in a radical and unusual light. He identified with his people. He ate, drank, spoke, was hungry and thirsty, ran out of money, became tired and died at the hands of occupying forces.

As Scripture points out, 'Since the children, as he calls them, are people of flesh and blood, Jesus himself became like them and shared their human nature. He did this so that, through his death, he might destroy the Devil who has the power over death, and in this way set free those who were slaves all their lives ...' (Heb 2:14–15).

This one true living God, the Creator of heaven and earth, of each and every universe and galaxy, really came to us. What is more, he still comes to be with us today. God actually wants to dwell in us, to live his life within ours. The apostle Paul makes it plain that from the moment we turn from living for ourselves and surrender the control of our lives to God a miracle occurs. He declares, 'God's Spirit lives in you' (Rom 8:9). Paul explains how this happens when he adds, 'God's Spirit joins himself to our spirits' (Rom 8:16).

It is this fact which clearly distinguishes Christianity from other faiths. Christianity offers what no other dare claim. Not just information about God, man and his world, not merely a set of standards to follow and a list of instructions to obey, but rather, an introduction to God. Instead of just telling us what to do, God supplies us with his Holy Spirit in order to provide us with the spiritual power by which we can live up to his standards. When we receive the forgiveness which Jesus died on a cross two thousand years ago to give us, God cleanses us from our sins and both qualifies and enables us to live as his sons and daughters.

God gives us his Spirit in order that we might be supernaturally equipped to live as God himself intended we should. This represents just about the only feasible explanation for how Rhoda can face her adverse circumstances but can still live, against all the odds, a truly triumphant life in Jesus.

This offer of God's living in us is one to which many, like Rhoda, have responded. God, far from being distant, now lives with us in the most intimate relationship possible. Many of us know this to be the truth because that is exactly what has happened in our own lives. But if we try to pretend that all has been straightforward from the start, we are guilty of putting our heads in the sand. A combination of unanswered questions married to fear and doubt inevitably raises problems in us all but, as time goes by, we forget the difficulties and simplify the situation so that it is often the case that experienced Christians tend to mislead new Christians into thinking all will be easy. They can also fail to emphasise the crucial importance of that relationship with the power and presence of God which is absolutely essential if we are to live the Christian life here on earth. The Holy Spirit has too often been the neglected Person of the Trinity. Nevertheless, his activity within each believer is a vital prerequisite if we are truly to engage in a fruitful relationship of service to God himself. It would be idiotic to suggest that we could be content with seeking to serve God in our own strength.

The plain and simple fact is that when it comes to living lives for God, we just cannot do it alone.

Chapter 2

Without the Spirit

A close friend was speaking to a group of Christian leaders at a large conference. He began to challenge them about the role of the Holy Spirit within their church communities. He concluded, as many others have done, that if the Spirit were to be taken from us, ninety-five per cent of our church activities would go on exactly as before. At the end of the session a question was asked. One of the leaders enquired how the local church could be structured so that the other five per cent could be covered as well!

The problem is that far too many of us have become suspicious of the Spirit. It is one of the tragedies of the Christian church within our nation that we have been so creative in devising ways and means of managing without the Holy Spirit. We have replaced him in so many areas of our lives with human resources and expertise. Instead of filling up at the petrol pump, we have concentrated on attempting to invent our own substandard bootleg fuel! Struggling to find means of coping alone, we have totally ignored God's magnificent provision for us.

The Christian life can never be reduced to the level of mere uniform obedience to a bunch of legal instructions nor is it possible to reduce it to the level of a set of routines or rituals which we are supposed slavishly to follow. Neither is it a process of obtaining some kind of esoteric 'secret' knowledge about humankind's destiny to rule the universe nor is it merely a process of coming to know ourselves better. These ideas only fall within the territories of other faiths. The claims of Christianity have always been much higher than such limited notions. For evangelical Christians, the message of the Christian faith is plain and direct, and it is revealed in the Bible. It can be briefly summarised in the affirmation that God came down to earth as a man, demonstrated what life could be and died on a cross to forgive and recover a people for himself.

Despite constant rejections throughout history, the living God has continued to stretch out his hands of love towards his people throughout the length and breadth of his world. As the Creator he loved enough to allow his son Jesus to die. Having broken out of the grave, Jesus now reigns at his Father's right hand in the glory of heaven. Now we eagerly wait for God's final act in history – taking his own people to be with him forever.

There is, however, one fundamental problem. Humankind has never fallen in with God's plans. We have consistently rejected God's will and purposes. God, however, wants all who have committed their lives to Jesus, and received his forgiveness, to spend eternity with him. And the Godhead does not just consist of the Father and the Son but is a Trinity of Father, Son and Holy Spirit.

The Holy Spirit is sent from within the Godhead as a divine gift to all who respond to the love of Jesus and own him as their Lord and King. He is given in order that we might keep growing in our Christian lives. His supreme purpose is to bear witness to Jesus and to prepare us for eternal life. He brings the life and power of Jesus into our lives in order that we too might become more like Jesus. Put simply, the Spirit-filled life of Jesus becomes ours, so he is the one who is at work within us, getting us ready for an eternal relationship with him.

This is God's gift of love, in that he recognises the fact that we cannot make it in our Christian lives without him. Instead of giving us some vague 'force', he equips us with his very own Spirit. But because the Holy Spirit is one with God the Father and God the Son, we need to come to a greater understanding of how this relationship within the Trinity works out. We will never comprehend it fully because our minds are only human. We can never expect fully to understand the Divine.

Augustine, one of the fathers of the early Church, wrote the earliest systematic treatment of the subject as part of his fifteen volume work *On the Trinity*. Since then most Christian scholars have agreed on these fundamental truths:

No person of the Trinity is superior or inferior to any other.

Christianity is not about three gods but about one God, for the Persons of the Trinity are one in nature and glory and work harmoniously for our salvation.

If all this sounds rather puzzling, don't worry. There are many things that we cannot grasp completely and, after all, if we knew all there was to know about God, he would hardly be worth knowing. The finite (we humans) were never intended to understand the infinite (God). If we could, our God would be reduced to human dimensions. He would be far too small.

Although God the Father took the initiative in creation, he did not create alone for the Son and Spirit were involved too. Neither does the Son or Spirit act alone. They are intimately bonded together in an eternal union so when the Holy Spirit comes into our lives, he does not enter alone. He always brings the Father and the Son with him.

When we pray, it is generally to the Father, through the Son, but in the Holy Spirit. To emphasise this threefold character of God, Paul delivered this simple blessing on the Corinthian church: 'The grace of the Lord Jesus Christ, the love of God, and the fellowship of the Holy Spirit be with you all' (2 Cor 13:14).

We have already said that we could not be expected to serve God properly if we were simply confined to our own limited human resources. So if we were without the Spirit, just where would we be?

There would be no uniqueness – there are so many religions and faiths which claim to bring information about God and man, past and future. For Christians, the Holy Spirit makes the difference. Instead of just talking about God – out there – we know him living within us! What is more, he is the Holy Spirit. The Greek word for 'holy' contains the meaning of being 'different'. He alone can take ordinary lives and work that transformation within them.

There would be no resurrection – without the Holy Spirit, Jesus would still be dead! Christianity would not even exist. The Holy Spirit is no optional extra but one of an undivided Trinity. Without the Spirit, not only would Jesus still be dead but we also would have no hope of having renewed bodies. 'If the Spirit of God, who raised Jesus from death, lives in you, then he who raised Christ from death will also give life to your mortal bodies by the presence of his Spirit in you' (Rom 8:11).

There would be no understanding – without the Spirit, we could not learn all that God longs to teach us. The Holy Spirit wants to share with us all that we need to know. He is uniquely qualified to do this because 'only God's Spirit knows all about God' (1 Cor 2:11).

There would be no life – the Spirit brings a quality of lifestyle which is its own testimony to the world in which God has placed us: ' ... to be controlled by the Spirit results in life and peace' (Rom 8:6).

There would be no obedience – something that only God can bring. As we live in obedience to his direction, we discover not an easy route but a God who never leaves us. 'Now, in obedience to the Holy Spirit, I am going ... the Holy Spirit has warned me that prison and troubles wait for me. But I reckon my own life to be worth nothing to me; I only want to complete my mission and finish the work that the Lord Jesus gave me to do' (Acts 20:22–24).

There would be no worship – without the Spirit, our worship would be little more than mere routine expression to God. As Jesus taught the Samaritan woman at the well, 'God is Spirit, and only by the power of his Spirit can people worship him as he really is' (John 4:24).

There would be no witness – without the Spirit, we would be left with only our own resources for serving Jesus and sharing his love with others. The disciples were told not even to attempt to do anything until they had received power from the Holy Spirit. 'But when the Holy Spirit comes upon you, you will be filled with power and you will be witnesses for me in Jerusalem, in all of Judea and Samaria and to the ends of the earth' (Acts 1:8).

There would be no gifts – without the Spirit, we could not receive from the Lord all that he wants to give to us in order that we might be properly equipped for his service. 'Whoever does not have the Spirit cannot receive the gifts that come from God's Spirit' (1 Cor 2:14).

There would be no power – challenged by God to live his life yet without being given the power to do so, all our Christian lives would amount to no more than the sum total of our maximum human exertion and efforts. The Holy Spirit introduces a totally different dimension, a source of power for living, which emanates from God himself in order to make us into radically different people. 'For the Spirit that God has given us does not make us timid; instead, his Spirit fills us with power, love and self-control' (2 Tim 1:7).

There would be no evidence – without the Spirit, we would have no supernatural events as a vivid demonstration of God's reality and power. These were never just the special province of the apostles. We read, for example, that 'Stephen, a man full of faith and the Holy Spirit ... a man richly blessed by God and full of power, performed great miracles and wonders among the people' (Acts 5:6,8).

There would be no guidance – without the Spirit, devoid of a real revelation of all that God has prepared for us, we would be stuck in the confines of our own ambitions. When, for example, Paul and his companions wanted to go into Bithynia, 'the Spirit of Jesus did not allow them' (Acts 16:7).

There would be no security – the Holy Spirit is God's guarantee to us that God can take care of us now and in the future. 'Because of the Spirit that God has given us, we know that God lives in union with us' (1 John 3:24). Time and again, the Holy Spirit is referred to as the Spirit of truth who fulfils God's promises to his people.

There would be no future – we have something to look forward to because we know that God 'has given us the Holy Spirit in our hearts as the guarantee of all that he has in store for us' (2 Cor 1:22).

To repeat the question, just where would we be without the Spirit? It is tragic that for so long many Christians have relegated the Holy Spirit to the fringes of their spiritual interest when there is so much that he has done for us, and wants to do within us. Little wonder that Satan has worked so hard to create division and confusion. Somehow he does not mind us having head knowledge about Jesus, just as long as he can prevent us enjoying the life of Jesus revealed by the

Holy Spirit within us. Satan would love us to neglect the Spirit!

Paul, James, Peter and John all write about the Holy Spirit in every letter except the two chapters of 2 and 3 John. They write of the fruit of the Spirit, the gifts of the Spirit, his work of guarding, resurrecting, witnessing, love-outpouring, renewing, interceding, demonstrating, gift-imparting, life-giving, transforming, sealing, promising, sanctifying, prophesying and Scripture-inspiring. How could we leave him out of our church life and teaching – indeed, in some cases, from many areas of our lives?

Sadly there are some who through lack of expectation have failed to experience all that the Holy Spirit wishes to do for them. They made a response to the love of Jesus but when they woke up the next morning, discovered that little seemed to have changed. The well-remembered promises of love and joy, to be accompanied by peace and satisfaction during every moment of their lives as Christians, now seemed to possess a hollow ring. The emotion of the moment, the experience, was undeniably real but what, if anything, had it all meant?

Tragically the lives of some Christians can indeed be something like this. Most of us would hate to admit it, but Christianity can have proved to be a little disappointing. The initial moment of commitment was so real, that instant of initial surrender to the claims of Jesus on our lives utterly genuine, but we missed out on the radical transformation which should have followed hard on the heels of our decision.

So we have struggled to keep our promises, but knowing about God has not proved adequate to enable us to live up to his standards. In fact, our Christian lives have resembled the two-thousand piece jigsaw which we started to put together only to discover that half the pieces were missing!

I well remember the time that, still a relatively young Christian, I began to question the reason for the inadequacies and failures in much of my Christian experience. I began to ask why it was that so many other Christians seemed to know more of the indwelling love of Jesus than I did? I could not help but wonder why it was that their lives seemed to display the fruits of his grace, and to demonstrate his power at work within them, in ways that were obviously lacking in me.

I soon found that I was not alone in my frustration. In fact, there were many others who felt just as I did. One such person was Bill. Bill would have called himself 'average'. In most ways he was just like the rest of us but when he committed his life to Jesus Christ, he began to feel that he was 'special' in the eyes of God. It all began with a glorious sense of joy that the living God should actually like him. He was really determined to serve the Lord. Friends told him that his constant sense of frustration and failure was quite usual but Bill knew that just couldn't be right. He tried so hard to do the things he knew God wanted and to ignore all temptation to do things he knew would hurt and offend Jesus, but instead of success his knowledge of his own personal failure continued to increase. The early joy faded and the bitterness of a pervasive sense of disappointment crept in. Somehow, for Bill, Christianity hadn't turned out to be all that Christians had claimed it to be.

It's so very easy to be horrified at such a suggestion but if God longs to live in our lives, why do many of us seem to end up so far away from him? Just look at the Christians around us. Though some have attractive lives, others seem boring or even downright obnoxious! Even if we allow for our own personal prejudices, there are still many unanswered questions!

As a new Christian, I found it even harder than I do now to understand how Christians could be so different from one another. Some overflowed with love and compassion for their neighbours while others locked themselves away for fear of contamination. Some seemed to exude a deep sense of inner joy while, in contrast, there were others who looked as if they had just received sentence of death rather than eternal life! Some were on fire with expectancy that God would do great things around them but others seemed totally indifferent, apparently content to make survival their prime objective. It all seemed so confusing.

At a personal level, the biggest struggle I faced as a young Christian lay in coming to grips with what I was expected to believe and experience concerning the Person and work of the

Holy Spirit. I began to encounter those for whom he was not a nebulous being. For such people, he had become readily identified as a vibrant, living reality within their lives, a person to know and love, not some vague generic force.

I had difficulty reconciling myself to the fact that I found it easier to identify with those who spoke in impersonal terms about the Holy Spirit. Yet many were engaged in making extravagant claims about the activity of the Holy Spirit in their own lives, and I began to wonder if I were losing out somewhere, or if others were simply deluding themselves. I knew that the Holy Spirit had taken up residence in my life. What then did I feel was missing? Perhaps there were dimensions of life in the Holy Spirit that I had yet to experience?

Could it be, perhaps, that I was lacking in some area of what it really meant to live in the power and authority of the Holy Spirit? I needed answers and I needed them immediately. When I started to ask for explanations for my lack of spiritual experience, I began to hear about the Holy Spirit. Immediately my suspicions were aroused. After all, I knew there was no one perspective about the Spirit's work. Each viewpoint challenged another and all this seemed to lead to was division, disagreement and dispute!

On the other hand I knew that this subject was vitally important, because some had even suggested that the differences in the way Christians lived could be directly attributed to the quality of their relationship with the Holy Spirit. I was certain that this had to be far too simple an explanation. Yet for myself, as for so many others, there had to be more to Christianity than mere belief. I had to find what it could really mean for God to live within me!

Chapter 3

Who is this Holy Spirit?

If we want to discover who the Holy Spirit really is, then individual human experience is not the right place to start. When God intended to reveal his nature, will and identity to humankind, he determined to do so supremely in his Son. When he wanted to place on record his activities with the inhabitants of this planet, he chose to do so in a book. If we want to know what the Spirit of God is like and how he operates within the lives of the people of God, then it is to the pages of the Bible that we must first turn.

It has been rightly pointed out that too many Christians have produced an artificial Trinity of Father, Son and Holy Scripture. But while the Bible is the Word of God, without error in all that it affirms, and is truly God-breathed, Scripture itself affirms that it is the Holy Spirit who is the third member of the Trinity.

Throughout the pages of the Bible it is always assumed that the Holy Spirit is no more and no less than God himself. He is called 'the Spirit of the Lord' (1 Kings 18:12), the gift of the Father (Luke 11:13), and 'the Spirit of Jesus' (Acts 16:7). Paul clearly announces, 'The Lord is the Spirit' (2 Cor 3:17). When Peter has to rebuke Ananias for his attempted deception he boldly announces the simple fact, 'You have lied to the Holy Spirit ... you have not lied to men but to God' (Acts 5:3,4). On the occasion that Jesus found himself speaking about the 'unforgivable sin', it was speaking against and rejecting not the Father or even Jesus himself but blasphemy against the Holy Spirit that was at stake (Matt 12:30–32). It is important to note that we can mock or curse our fellow human beings but blasphemy is a sin that can only be committed against God himself.

It is because the Holy Spirit is God that Scripture describes him as possessing all those essential hallmarks, which are the sole privilege of God himself. He is:

Holy – God cannot deny his own character; therefore in the same way that God is completely pure and totally unblemished, so must be his 'Holy' Spirit (1 Cor 6:19).

Eternal – if God were limited by time and space, he could not, by definition, be God. The Creator can neither be limited by his creation nor die or face extinction. These ideas are nonsense if applied to the living God. To be God, he must always have been God and must inhabit eternity. When Scripture says that the Holy Spirit is eternal (always was, and always will be), then it is actually affirming that he is God (Heb 9:14).

Omnipotent – he is all-powerful, an attribute that is the sole province of God himself (Luke 1:35–37).

Omnipresent – he exists everywhere simultaneously. There is no part of heaven, earth, or the universe that is not inhabited by the Holy Spirit (Ps 139:7).

Omniscient – the Holy Spirit simply knows everything that there is to know (1 Cor 2:10–11).

These supreme qualities of the Holy Spirit are neatly summarised in Isaiah's prophecy where he predicts the character and virtues of the anticipated Messiah in these words,

'The Spirit of the Lord will rest upon him –
the Spirit of wisdom and understanding,
the Spirit of counsel and power,
the Spirit of knowledge and the fear of the Lord' (Isa 11:2).

God is personal. He neither rules nor communicates by remote control and he possesses personality. These truths must therefore equally apply to the Holy Spirit. It would be wrong to view him as some kind of indefinably nebulous 'force'. Too often we can be tempted to regard the Holy Spirit as some vague kind of divine 'it'. This would be far from the truth. For God the Father refers to him as 'My Spirit' (Gen 6:3; Isa 59:21).

He is the 'breath' or 'wind' of God (Isa 40:7). In the New Testament, the Greek word employed is *pneuma*, which does literally have these two meanings. It is hard to see how this word could not but refer to something broad and vague. Yet Scripture often brings into grammatical play the definite article. So instead of 'a breath' or 'a wind', he is called 'the Spirit' or 'the Holy Spirit'. His person-hood is also affirmed in that he can be grieved (Eph 4:30), comes upon individuals at particular times, is the means by which God fills his people and can even be withdrawn from them under exceptional circumstances (Judg 14:6; 2 Kings 2:9; Exod 35:31; Mic 3:8; Ps 51:11).

The Holy Spirit is no mere arm or leg of God. He is a Person, yet he exists as part of the Godhead. He is not remote but actually dwells in God's people. He is therefore personal to each one of us. It is to reinforce this point that the Apostle John refers to the Holy Spirit by using a masculine pronoun (*ekeinos* = he) to accompany a neuter noun (*pneuma* = spirit). This may seem like bad grammar, but it is certainly superb theology because he does this in order to emphasise that the Holy Spirit is a 'he', not an 'it' (see John 14: 26; 15:26; 16:8-14).

The Holy Spirit is not only personal, he also possesses a unique personality. The three key characteristics of basic personality lie in our innate capacity for feeling, knowing and doing – you may be surprised to learn that the Holy Spirit is personally and actively engaged in all three! Scripture affirms that:

He feels (Eph 4:30).

He knows (John 14:26).

He does things (John 16:8-11).

While it is important to note that the Holy Spirit is like us in possessing personality, it is also important to recognise that, unlike us, he is in fact 'holy'. The Greek word used is *hagios*, and its root meaning is 'different'. In this sense, he can never be as we are and it is just one demonstration of the grace and mercy of God that he allows his 'Holy' Spirit to dwell in unclean and intrinsically evil human beings. The very title 'Holy Spirit' indicates that this Spirit is totally different from us because he is, in fact, divine.

While God is one he exists as Trinity (Matt 28:19; John 14:26, 15:26; 2 Cor 13:14; 1 Pet 1:2).

Jesus reveals this supreme mystery of the Christian faith when he declares the name of God into which his followers should be baptised. The word used for 'name' is singular because there is only one God, but this name is tri-personal because each one of us is baptised in 'the name of the Father and of the Son and of the Holy Spirit' (Matt 28:19).

In Revelation, John begins his letter to the seven churches an unusual way, by greeting them in a manner that places God the Father first, God the Son third and God the Spirit second (Rev 1:4,5). While the order might be unusual, the phraseology is standard because, time and again, the Scriptures refer to the Godhead as existing in three Persons. The implication is inevitable that these three must be regarded as being inextricably intertwined and always co-equal.

Because we do find it more difficult to visualise and personalise the Holy Spirit, we can often overlook the amount of work in which the Holy Spirit is engaged. It would not be irreverent to say that he is very busy indeed. The Holy Spirit is definitely multi-tasked, for while he is the corporate Holy Spirit of the universal Church (1 Cor 12:13), he is also the one who dwells in the life of every individual believer (Rom 8:9–11).

The Holy Spirit is always busy. He works within us to bring conviction of sin, recognition of the need for righteousness and an awareness of impending judgement long before a person comes to the point of conversion and surrenders his or her life to Jesus Christ (John 16:8). It is the Holy Spirit who is already at work in their lives, getting them ready for just that moment, as in the New Testament accounts of the conversions of Zacchaeus, Cornelius and that unnamed eunuch who served Queen Candace as Ethiopia's Chancellor of the Exchequer. It was the Holy Spirit who was actively at work preparing the ground for their moments of truth. In the Chancellor's case, he even had to call Philip away from a revival to get him to the desert to explain the Scriptures to him!

When we come to Christ, the Holy Spirit comes to make his home in the life of each and every believer. He is the giver of new life, and becomes the seal and evidence of our salvation (see John 3:5; 2 Cor 1:22; Titus 3:5; and especially Rom 8:9–11). Subsequently it is the Holy Spirit who has to take on the 'raw material' of the new convert and begin the process, often lengthy, of seeking to make each one of us more and more like our Lord Jesus. This whole idea of an indwelling Holy Spirit, who inhabits the life of every believer, introduced to planet Earth a concept unknown in other major world religions. For the first time, we were not to be introduced to a set of principles or beliefs concerning a God who was 'out there' somewhere, but instead, to a God who could be known, loved and served right here and now. This Christianity was offering not a religion about God, but a relationship with him.

Time and again I have had the privilege of watching this being worked out in practice. This has usually been at its most obvious in the lives of the poorest of the poor and of those who live and work among them.

Silviane lives in Haiti. She was only sixteen years old when she was raped. The perpetrator of the abuse was the man for whom she worked as a domestic servant. She left the house but two or three months later, discovered to her horror that she was pregnant as a result of the rape. After the birth, and now with a child to look after, she found that the only way to survive was through prostitution. She would sell her body for ten Haitian gourdes, about a pound. The inevitable result was more children from unknown fathers. The end of that chapter in her story was that she found it necessary to work the streets all day long in order to feed her little family.

After six years of having to live in this fashion, Silviane was occupying a little shack in a vast slum which served as 'home' for several thousand of Haiti's poorest people. This notorious area was adjacent to the headquarters of the Lemuel project, an indigenous evangelical organisation set up to offer care and support for those living in such squalid conditions. Its Director, a warm and approachable Haitian named Manis, has a simple rule for the staff involved with the project. He insists that there is to be no verbal attempt at direct evangelism until people are first asking questions for themselves. His conviction is that Christian lives should provoke questions not by what we avoid but by what we do.

So evangelism in this community has its starting point in the interest created from what the people have witnessed in the compassionate concern and active care for others which typifies the lives of these Christians. The only exception Manis feels obliged to make to his rule is for those suffering from AIDS and others who are chronically sick. Those who just may not have enough time left are told of Jesus immediately.

Gigi Munchmore, an American nurse who has lived in Haiti for thirty-seven years, met and befriended Silviane. After several months, she was eventually asked the bitter and honest question, 'What are you trying to get from me?' The answer came back that instead of wanting to exploit Silviane, Gigi was trying to give her something. She led her to commit her life to Jesus.

Today, Silviane's home is still the same tiny and primitive hut in the shanty-town in Port-au-Prince. The entire dwelling consists of a single room, which she shares with her five children. Because Silviane is given to hospitality, and is reluctant to see people with absolutely nowhere to go, at times as many as eight people will live in that one room 'constructed' from discarded pieces of used plywood or tin. We can only imagine Silviane's delight on the day she discovered her pride and joy, a freshly discarded quite new section of a sheet of tin, which actually had no holes in it! Joining in the weekly small-group fellowship meeting, she wanted everyone to share her joy and thank the Lord with her. The reason for her excitement was that she at last had a small corner of her room where she could sit and not get wet when it rained.

Many of us would want to ask what it is that could possibly have made such a difference in the lives of Manis, Silviane and Gigi.

How can Silviane be so happy at receiving so little?

How can Gigi be content to find her mission field in one of the worst slums on earth?

How can the message of Jesus be expressed without words?

How can Christians find the joy of Jesus when living in such appalling conditions?

The answer can only lie in a supernatural power, in God himself. In plain and simple fact, the Holy Spirit has done this.

The kind of Christian life that is introduced by the Holy Spirit is one in which he does the work; we just cooperate. Instead of being satisfied with producing a recital of aspirations that we are supposed to live up to or a list of commands that we are compelled to attempt to obey, the Christian experiences that God has himself supplied us with the means to live up to his own demands. He has given us his Holy Spirit (Rom 8). The Spirit is actively working on, through and in our lives. Ultimately what will emerge is a transformed character which will stand in sharp contrast to that of a person who can only attempt to live life in God's world, but without God.

The result will be seen in a radically changed lifestyle. This is witnessed through the pervasive demonstration of the fruit of the Holy Spirit in the life of the believer. Love, joy peace, patience, kindness, goodness, faithfulness, gentleness and self-control (Gal 5:22,23) do not arrive in separate packages but are all part and parcel of the same character transformation. Many have recognised that this is, in fact, all one fruit. It just comes in nine different flavours. Just because we have patience, it does not mean that we should be content to condemn ourselves to a war-like existence. Exhibiting unusual patience in no way implies that we are not intended to enjoy the Spirit's peace as well.

The presence of the Holy Spirit in our lives determines the fact that we are intended to demonstrate each aspect of the Spirit's fruit in equal measure. This will be recognised in the different ways that the Holy Spirit is seen to be at work in our lives and in our world. The briefest glance makes the enormous size and scope of his workload become obvious. It includes:

Working in Creation (Gen 1:2; Job 33:4).

Transmitting creative skills to human beings (Exod 31:1–11; 1 Kings 7:14).

Inspiring and revealing truth (1 Sam 10:10; John 16:13).

Bringing the reality of the Father to us (Rom 8:15).

Glorifying Jesus (John 16:14), and making him real to us (Acts 7:55).

As God, always dwelling in the lives of us as individuals (Rom 8:9), and as the body of Christ (1 Cor 2:12).

Bringing us conviction of sin and providing us with the power to overcome it (John 16:8–10; Rom 8:13).

Bringing out of the depths of our beings our own response to God in the light of his love for us (Ps 51:10–12; Ezek 36:25–27; Joel 2:28–29).

Assuring each one of us of the permanence and security of our relationship with Jesus (Rom 8:16).

Helping us to anticipate the future life (2 Cor 5:5).

Strengthening us (Eph 3:16), and filling our lives (Acts 4:31; Eph 5:18).

Providing instruction, and confirming the truth of God to us (Acts 11:12; John 15:26; 1 Cor 2:12).

Giving leadership (Ps 143:10; Acts 13:2; Rom 8:14).

Removing fear (2 Tim 1:7).

Praying and engaging in spiritual warfare through us (Eph 6:17,18).

Controlling the course of both nature and human history (Ps 104:29,30; Isa 34:16; 40:7).

We may well be tempted to wonder at how it is that God can reside in each one of us simultaneously. Surely he must have to divide up his Holy Spirit in order to make this possible? The simple answer is that this is not necessary. As one perceptive twentieth-century voice observed, 'An infinite God can give all of himself to each of his children. He does not distribute himself that all may have a part, but to each he gives all of himself as fully as if there were no others' (A W Tozer, *The Divine Conquest*, OM Publishing, 1979).

In other words, we do not even have to share the Holy Spirit with others. We can each possess all of him that there is to have. Everywhere we go, we are assured of the presence of the Holy Spirit (Ps 139:7). He becomes the controlling influence of God within us and acts as our guide and spiritual director. He empowers us for service and he instructs us in all that we need to know. The Holy Spirit is the deposit and guarantee of eternal life. He acts as the promise of all that is to come and he stays with us forever. In the light of all this, it becomes less surprising that Jesus assured his disciples of how it would be to their advantage for him to go away, because then his Spirit would come.

And it is indeed his Spirit.

For Jesus was conceived by the Holy Spirit, and born in order that he might perform the will of the Father (Luke 1:32–35). Immediately following his own baptism, Jesus was anointed by the Holy Spirit at the same time that the Father spoke to the observers of the scene from heaven (Matt 3: 16–17). The ministry of the Holy Spirit was to reveal Jesus to men and women, and he would, in turn, show his Father to them (John 14:9,26). This same Holy Spirit was to be Christ's own gift to all believers, enabling them to live in the way that he intended for them, fulfilling the mission that he had given to them (Acts 2:32–33).

One of the single most baffling questions of human history lies in trying to explain how it was that 120 frightened, cowering people, barely hanging onto their own existence, could be suddenly transformed into an army of men and women who would effectively turn their world upside down. One moment they were huddling together for survival, the next they were venturing outside their closed walls in order to change the destiny of humankind. Armed with no weapons other than their own naked confidence in the will of God, they persuaded the inhabitants of the Roman empire to believe their conviction that a dead carpenter was alive and had opened the doors of forgiveness and eternity to all who would surrender the control of their lives into his nail-pierced hands.

Their lives pre-dated the eras of air transport, information technology and global communication. Travelling mainly by foot, progress was frustratingly slow. Regularly they faced the perils of bandits or disease, constantly risking life and limb to the dangers of shipwreck and always knowing that hostile authorities lay at the end of their journey. They were experiencing torture, imprisonment and death, yet no persecution could extinguish the brightness of their flame. Standing up to proclaim truth in the marketplace, freely gossiping the gospel to colleagues and entrusting to cumbersome rolls of parchment their message of eternal life, painfully but indelibly scratched out by quill pen, these were not members of a cult which would swiftly die out. Indeed, as the early church historian Tertullian observed towards the close of the second century AD, 'The blood of the martyrs is the seed of the Church'.

So how did it happen? What mysterious event took place among people who lived some two thousand years ago in order to usher in a movement that would today incorporate an active membership of more than 1,000 million people? No human analysis can even begin to explain how these events could possibly have happened in the dramatic way that they did. The story almost requires supernatural intervention to become believable – and that is exactly what happened.

Because they were now living as those within whose lives the Holy Spirit had taken up permanent residence, these early Christians were able to set out boldly to go where nobody had gone before. Gripped by a message of God's transforming love, they began to seek to win this lost world back for Jesus. This is exactly what the Holy Spirit does. Because of who he is, he makes ordinary people into the very hands and feet of Jesus. As God himself, he is always seeking to shape the lives of God's people and to lift up our heads to appreciate and glory in the full majesty of the Godhead.

Thus a new way was to begin at Pentecost. Because of the offering by Jesus of himself on a cross, a new chapter opened in the story of God's dealings with humankind. The Holy Spirit simply took hold of the lives of a group of ordinary people. He began to work at transforming them from what they were into what they could become. The result was to be men, women and children who, by virtue of the power of the Holy Spirit at work within their lives, had begun to be changed. They were beginning to see God at work both in and through their lives.

So who then is this Holy Spirit? He is God at work in us, progressively making us more and more like Jesus. For this is what the Holy Spirit can accomplish through some very raw material. He takes hold of ordinary people and makes us into those he can use to be responsible for transforming both the history of the world and the population of heaven.

Chapter 4

Receiving the Spirit

What could be easier? Jesus promised his disciples that he would not leave them as orphans. So at the very moment in which we surrender our lives in commitment to Jesus Christ, he invades our lives with his Holy Spirit. Finis! Next chapter?

Yes, but why then do so many sincere born-again Christians find that later in their Christian experience, they begin to plead for a deeper experience of God than they knew at first, while others seem to receive all they need at the point of their initial conversion. It is here that evangelical Christians will usually begin to disagree with each other. It seems that differing belief about the role of the Holy Spirit in the life of individual Christians has been their biggest single cause of internal division over the past thirty years.

The epicentre of this controversy is located in the term 'baptism with the Holy Spirit'. The question relates to whether or not this can refer to a one-off instantaneous experience at some time after an individual has repented and been united with God through the Holy Spirit. If this is possible, then the second question emerges as to whether this is an essential spiritual experience for all believers. If it is, we need to ask if some are right in their insistence that the necessary evidence for this 'baptism' is that one immediately speaks in other tongues.

Faced with a smorgasbord of choices

'Then he breathed on them and said, "Receive the Holy Spirit"' (John 20:22). When Jesus said something it certainly happened. But only a few weeks later, those eleven disciples were among a crowd of 120 believers who received a mighty baptism in the Holy Spirit. They then began to speak in other tongues and went out to turn their world upside down! So we are left enquiring whether that is the same experience that we need for today.

Jesus received that same kind of anointing for service at his baptism, not with tongues of fire because there was no sin in him to be purged, but with a gentle dove. Anglican clergymen, friends of mine, have received a baptism with tongues of fire. Hundreds of thousands of Christians have received a mighty baptism with the Holy Spirit and have then begun to speak in tongues. Yet many who have received that gift from God have not turned their world upside down and many who have no such claim to that kind of experience have contributed mighty ministries to the body of Christ and the world in which they live. While there is often, in Scripture and in the experience of many today, a connection between receiving a special anointing of the Spirit and speaking in tongues, not every incidence in Scripture or in the experience of many has produced the same connection.

Others have claimed to receive the same kind of baptism in the Holy Spirit, but in much quieter fashion. Drawing comfort from the apostle who could confidently assert, 'I thank God that I speak in tongues much more than any of you' (1 Cor 14:18), they argue that he grew into the gift, because Luke makes no such claim that Paul exercised this gift at the same moment he was filled with the Spirit.

A further viewpoint challenges the whole claim that we need a specific 'one-off' experience of the Holy Spirit. Attention is drawn to Paul's emphasis on the need for us to go on being sanctified by the Holy Spirit. It is claimed that, although we do not attain all God's ultimate standards for our lives at the moment of conversion, we do receive all that we might need in order to achieve those standards. Besides which, it is pointed out, our concentration should surely be upon Jesus rather than the Holy Spirit!

Filled in different ways

The problem is that there is real truth in each of these arguments. The history of the Church serves to show that each viewpoint has always had its adherents – sometimes few, sometimes many. So at least we are not alone in our confusion! The major alternative views that have been suggested about the 'baptism in the Holy Spirit' are:

Spiritual regeneration and our baptism with the Holy Spirit coincide with our baptism in water.

Individual conversion is a 'once and for all' event. This is followed by a gradual work of sanctification (making us more like Jesus) which is initiated and carried through in individual lives by the Holy Spirit. This is the view which has traditionally been associated with 'non-charismatic evangelicals'. They maintain that, at the time of conversion, every Christian receives all the empowering that he or she needs. All that is then required is its consistent outworking in the life of the believer. Any 'crisis' is simply one of the many close encounters that an individual may have with God during his or her spiritual journey

This baptism is a sealing in our lives by the Holy Spirit who brings the confirmation of the assurance of our personal salvation.

While the Holy Spirit is fully received at the moment of conversion, the latent potential is only fully experienced at a subsequent moment of spiritual release.

The baptism in the Holy Spirit is usually a second or subsequent experience following personal conversion. It normally takes the form of a crisis experience and introduces the believer to new dimensions of worship, faith, and the use of spiritual gifts. It is above all a furnishing of power, which is designed to make the believer more effective in Christian service.

Another view follows the same outline as the previous one, but insists on the use of the gift of tongues as the 'initial evidence' that this baptism has been received. These last two views represent the Pentecostal evangelical perspective. Here the emphasis is on the need for the Christian to receive a crisis experience in the Holy Spirit that will usually come some time after her conversion. This will then provide the believer with a gateway leading towards deeper intimacy in her relationship with God, greater potential for victory over ongoing sins in her life, a stronger sense of personal emotional freedom and more release in worship alongside the reception and use of spiritual gifts. This is certainly an extravagant and desirable 'hit list'; it is only fair to point out that an initial 'gateway' indicates the beginning, rather than the end, of the journey towards spiritual discovery.

We must be very careful to avoid insisting that everyone else needs to follow the same spiritual path by which God has led us as individuals. It is always vital to remember that to demand all others should be like us is probably an indication of our personal insecurity rather than of divine intention. For the living God is perfectly able to lead his people by different routes to the same destination. The same caution should also apply to our use of words. In the New Testament, the term 'baptism in the Holy Spirit' is often associated with repentance and faith as part of the conversion experience. Since then, many Christians who have come to a deeper experience of the Spirit after their conversion have referred to that experience as a 'baptism in the Holy Spirit'. Because we use words in different ways, the danger is that we fail to understand each other.

We tend too easily to interpret Scripture in the light of our own personal experience. This leads to false feelings of spiritual superiority, as we then assume that we must be right and therefore everyone else is simply wrong. This is a very dangerous practice because it means that we place the power and intentions of God within the very narrow box of our own understanding. Often, instead of allowing others the liberty to search for that biblical experience of the Spirit which God has made available for them, we try to lead them into an experience that mimics our own.

Charismatic evangelicals and non-charismatic evangelicals have this in common: they share an evangelical heritage that unites them in faith and experience in all areas other than an understanding of the person and work of the Holy Spirit. However, having seen where we can differ, let us now turn to examine where, even on this issue, we have areas of surprisingly broad agreement.

Evangelical Christians all agree that each one of us needs power from God with which to live the Christian life. In our own human strength, we cannot meet the demands that Jesus placed on the lifestyle of his disciples. The attitudes required and the challenges involved in the Christian life are beyond us. We cannot cope alone.

Our words, life, prayer, compassion, witness – all are woefully inadequate. That is why the disciples were forbidden to go out as missionaries before the Day of Pentecost (see Acts 1:4). The result would have been an overwhelming spiritual disaster. In the same way we need the Holy Spirit to use our lives as containers for himself. Then the words, life, prayer, compassion, even the witness, come from God himself.

That power is available to all God's people because each of us receives the Holy Spirit at conversion as the promise of all that he longs to achieve in each one of us.

The fulfilment of that divine potential is so often hindered by those basic weaknesses that must be removed by the Holy Spirit before he can do a full and complete work in us. Self-doubt, insecurity, guilt, anxiety and sin are always the prime target for his divine activity. We tend to despise ourselves, but the Holy Spirit longs to reveal to us the reality that we are God's creation and that he has never devised useless creatures. Our feelings of personal inadequacy can only be removed by his gentle touch.

He longs to cleanse and release us from our failure. At the very moment we recognise our inability to do the will of God, we can surrender to the Holy Spirit the right to replace our feeble human struggles with a divine power and initiative, which no power on earth could ever duplicate. When we then realise that, by his Spirit, Jesus can achieve all things within us, we discover the glorious freedom of allowing him to be God in us!

The Holy Spirit wants to achieve more in our lives than a mere one-off experience. Paul's words to the Ephesian church, 'be filled', were both a command and an instruction. More literally translated, they read, 'be being filled'. In other words, they speak of a daily, ongoing release. If we are trying to live today in the strength of any past experience, be it conversion or a later filling of the Spirit, we will only be disappointed.

The famed American evangelist Dwight L Moody was once speaking to a nineteenth-century British congregation on this theme and some, particularly among the leaders and clergy, were offended by his words. Moody was taken to one side after the meeting and interrogated. 'Why do you say that we need to go on being filled with the Holy Spirit – we've been filled, twenty or thirty years ago. Why do we need to be filled again?'

Moody's reply was a classic of spiritual common sense: 'I need to be filled with the Spirit every moment of each day because I leak!' We are still a very leaky people who desperately need to know the reality of God in our experience today - not just in our memories!

A sense of holy dissatisfaction with the poverty of our knowledge of God and our love for him would quickly transform the situation. No longer would we be content with merely knowing about God, we would hunger to know God, and not just by hearsay! In other words, we would demand a deep, intimate relationship. The Holy Spirit himself prompts that very desire in our hearts.

The Holy Spirit brings more than gifts to the people of God; he produces fruit in our lives. That is why, in Galatians 5:22, Paul speaks of one fruit but nine flavours – love, joy, peace, patience, kindness, goodness, faithfulness, humility and self-control (Gal 5:22,23). They must always lie at the heart of the Christian life.

Every major passage in the New Testament on the subject of gifts (1 Cor 12; Rom 12; Eph 4; 1 Pet 4) is accompanied by a passage on fruit. This is because fruit and gifts are not alternatives but co-essentials. The effective exercise of spiritual gifts depends upon the fruit of the Spirit. The Corinthian church tried to use one without the other and became a spiritual disaster area. As Peter Wagner says, 'Gifts without fruit are like a car tyre without air - the ingredients are all there, but they are worthless.'

Fruit-bearing for beginners

When it comes to the subject of bearing fruit for Jesus in our daily lives, most of us will simply feel like raw beginners. Yet the good news is that we are not condemned to seeking to achieve this on our own. For here is a life-style which the Spirit of God wants to create among the disciples of Jesus. Nor is there one single stereotype to which everyone must conform. We will all still be different but there will be common characteristics that emerge from the fruit that he brings to birth in our lives.

One important fact to realise is that it is impossible to produce the fruit of the Spirit on our own. If I pray to grow in patience I can expect God to send somebody into my life who's difficult to get on with, so that I have plenty of opportunities to practise being patient! It's in the business of everyday life that the Spirit will gradually change us to be more caring, kind, reliable – like Jesus.

We will never be able to produce spiritual fruit by our own good resolutions or self-effort. It is a natural process, as fruit-bearing always is. After all, when did you last see an apple tree in the middle of an orchard struggling for breath, writhing in agony, and screaming to produce 'apples ... pips ... cores?' Yet many Christians seem to try to please God by this kind of process!

What does an apple tree require in order to grow and produce fruit? It needs sunlight, roots, and moisture. Then growth becomes a natural process. In the same way if we are open to the sunlight of God's love, rooted in our relationship with him through the Bible and prayer, and also relaxing in the fullness of his Spirit, then growth and fruit are inevitable.

The problem for so many of us is that we are still trying too hard! We suffer from our vanity, which demands that we must play a significant part in God's divine activities within our lives. Our insecurity shouts that all must follow the same spiritual pathway that we do ... our fears compel us to strive, and go on striving. But the truth is that all our self-effort will never produce spiritual fruit because that is the prerogative of the Holy Spirit alone.

Yet despite all these areas of agreement the doctrine of the Person and work of the Holy Spirit remains at the centre of one of the greatest controversies that the church has faced in Western Europe during this century. Brother has been set against brother, denominations divided, churches split and in some cases their witness destroyed. Individual Christians have limped along, seeking one spiritual experience after another.

Argument and debate have proved inconclusive; as A W Tozer has put it, 'an enemy has done this ... Satan has opposed the doctrine of the Spirit-filled life about as bitterly as any other doctrine there is. He has confused it, opposed it, surrounded it with false notions and fears. He has blocked every effort of the Church of Christ to receive from the Father her divine and blood-bought patrimony. The church has tragically neglected this great liberating truth – that there is now, for the child of God, a full and wonderful and completely satisfying anointing with the Holy Ghost.'

For those who need a crisis!

The growth of the charismatic or Pentecostal emphasis in the church has proved to be astounding. Chile, Brazil, Colombia and Korea are outstanding examples of spiritual growth. The twentieth century was labelled as 'the era of the Holy Spirit' and certainly a new emphasis has come on the need to 'know God' in reality.

The question is – how?

Faced with that question, many have withdrawn to the safe ground of their own experience of God. Yet time and again, Scripture shows God working in a variety of ways to answer individual needs. Only one thing is ultimately quite certain and this is that God does want all his people to be filled with his Spirit. But how he does it – that is a matter best left for each of us to determine under his direction rather than our own inclination.

Begin to ask Jesus to fill you with his Holy Spirit. If he assures you in your heart that he's done that already – then keep going! If he does not, then:

Present yourself (Rom 12:1,2).

Ask (Luke 11:9–11).

Obey (Acts 5:32).

Have faith (Gal 3:2).

Don't set God an agenda to which he must operate and don't resist those gifts which he would then give you. Neither be afraid to speak in tongues if the Lord encourages you in that direction nor condemn yourself if you don't. If you still feel uncertain or unclear, don't hesitate to go to a mature Christian who can help. Remember that Paul had to wait for Ananias to come and lay hands on him and we ourselves may need to receive the laying on of hands as the visible, external sign that the living God is at work within us. So many of us need a trigger – personally, I will never forget four o'clock in the morning on a certain day. I was leading a mission at a small south coast church, yet I knew that I also needed a touch from God. I remember what it was like, after the Lord had torn me apart through the witness of a university student on my team, to admit my need and recognise for the first time that I needed help. I had to acknowledge that I could not get through on my own. I asked that student to pray for me; he and his girlfriend laid hands on my head and prayed, 'Father, I don't even know why we're doing this but it was done in Scripture so we're copying. Please empty Clive and fill him; flood his whole life with your Holy Spirit.'

That morning, nearly three decades ago, saw the beginning of a whole new chapter in my own spiritual experience. I did not receive all God had for me, but I began to enjoy more of what was mine in Christ. I started discovering new things and, above all, finding a new reality in my relationship with Jesus.

You see, each one of us is very like a hotel, full of many different rooms, one for each aspect of our lives. God wants to empty each of those rooms, clean them out and move in to inhabit them for himself. But we so often want to limit the areas of our lives in which we are prepared to allow God to rule and to reign. So often we fall into the trap of trying to confine the sovereign Lord himself to just one room – and that can never be sufficient.

God wants us to learn that apart from his Spirit we can achieve nothing. 'I don't do the good I want to do' (Rom 7:19). We could never allow ourselves just to go on sinning in order that God's forgiveness might be multiplied. J B Phillips's version of Paul's reply must be an Englishman's classic, 'What a ghastly thought!' Instead, we need to recognise our need to be, each day, filled with the Holy Spirit. Why do we possess such a basic need? It is so that we might each learn to live in God's strength rather than in our own. It is not so that we might automatically become sinless but so that we may learn to sin less and less and less!

For too long we have hidden in fear from that simple but basic and life-transforming thing which God wants to do within each one of us. Yet this is far from an original thought! J I Brice once pointedly remarked that 'the Church has halted somewhere between Golgotha and Pentecost.' Another preacher, Rufus Mosely, has commented on his belief that 'the average spiritual temperature in the church is so low that when a healthy man comes along everyone thinks he has a fever.' Leonard Ravenhill succinctly summarised the problem when he pointed out the way in which 'when warned of false fire by fireless men, we so often settle for no fire at all.'

If we are to see a major move of God in our nation then that work will begin in individual lives. If we are to challenge our society with the good news of the Jesus they reject then we must discover a new power from outside ourselves. The source of that power lies within God himself. The Holy Spirit lies at the very heart of our mission. He is the 'helper' who God has given to us. He is our guide who not only points out the direction for us to go but actually wants to take us there.

There is a danger that because we know these truths so well, we might find that our very familiarity could breed contempt. We must never forget that the one who dwells in our lives is no less a Person than the Holy Spirit of the living God. We should always remember that Jesus sternly forbade sinning against his Spirit and that the Apostle Paul warned us of the danger of grieving the Holy Spirit. In the Old Testament, he was even sometimes withdrawn from those who had once known his power. Now that Jesus has bequeathed his Spirit to us, we have the guarantee that he will never be removed. But this does not mean that we should ever just take the Holy Spirit for granted. We must always be ready and willing to allow him to move us on.

One could almost imagine Paul raising his index finger in order to admonish the church in Thessaloniki as he wrote these words, 'Do not put out the Spirit's fire' (1 Thess 5:19, NIV). We need to take on board that same warning for today – and let the fire burn!

To some of us, the call will come simply to humble ourselves and pray; others will need to seek ministry and help. The end result must be the same – lives filled and renewed by the Spirit of God. Then, and only then, will people recognise what they saw in those early disciples – the life of Jesus reflected in his people. For that is the reason the Holy Spirit has been given, not to point in his own direction but to draw the attention of everyone who is prepared to look towards Jesus.

Some years ago I was conducting a mission in a city on the south coast. During the mission, I met a roly-poly, cheerful individual named Charlie. He was a university post-graduate student and a pillar of the local church, twenty-two years old and quite a mature Christian. One night, Charlie came to see me with tears in his eyes: 'Clive,' he asked, 'I want a straight answer to a straight question.'

'Okay, fire ahead,' I replied.

'Why, when non-Christians took note that the early church had been with Jesus, do none of my friends seem to see Jesus in me?'

That is a question which only Jesus can answer, so we knelt and prayed together that he would take every part of Charlie's life and fill him then, and from then onwards, with his Holy Spirit. Afterwards I heard this story. Two days later, when Charlie was working in a laboratory with a Pakistani fellow-student, he was asked, 'Charlie, what happened to you forty-eight hours ago? You're a different kind of Charlie!'

Years later, he still is! Quite a number of non-Christians have met Jesus because they first saw him living in Charlie. A generation of 'Charlies' is the crying need of the day, but that starts with you - and me - and Jesus! Lives that the Holy Spirit touched and entered at conversion need to be filled by him if we are to live God's way in God's world so that our neighbours and colleagues may begin again to recognise the reign of God within the lives of his people.

Chapter 5

Anointed – for what?

Every day, we witness to the saving love of Jesus and the transforming power of his Spirit in our lives. We can only live and
speak as the Spirit enables us. But God also intends his people
to demonstrate his power in the world. He calls us to specific
acts of ministry and service which demand a special empowering from the Holy Spirit.

Throughout the Old Testament, we read about the Holy
Spirit coming 'upon' people to prepare them for service. In the
New Testament, the Holy Spirit comes to live within the lives
of God's people.

This distinction between the Holy Spirit coming 'in' or 'on'
a person is not complete. The Holy Spirit came 'on' the 120
believers at the Day of Pentecost. It was in the authority of that
anointing that they then moved out and turned their world
upside down.

The Holy Spirit may well live 'within' us but he still comes
'upon' us to anoint our lives for particular acts of service.
Whereas his presence within us is permanent, his anointing on
us is not. Four times we read that the Spirit of God came 'on'
Samson (Judg 13:25; 14:6,19; 15:14), but then came the fateful
day when 'he did not know that the Lord had left him' (Judg
16:20). Through his disobedience and lack of commitment, he
had lost the power of the Spirit. Saul forfeited that anointing.

David, who succeeded Saul as King of Israel, was
panic-stricken when his adultery with Bathsheba and subsequent murder of her husband were exposed. He was terrified at
the thought that the same could happen to him. That is why
he pleaded with God, 'Do not take your Holy Spirit away from
me' (Ps 51:11).

Without that anointing, our labours for God can never
attain their full potential. Day by day, we need to know the
Holy Spirit's filling and anointing on our lives. Then, and only

then, can we join Jesus in saying, 'The Spirit of the Lord is upon me, because he has chosen me to bring good news to the poor. He has sent me to proclaim liberty to the captives and recovery of sight to the blind; to set free the oppressed and announce that the time has come when the Lord will save his people' (Luke 4:18,19).

Anointed to live a new life

It is at this point that so many new believers encounter incredible difficulties. It is great to be the recipients of a divine salvation but from what are we really supposed to be saved? What is this new life into which the Holy Spirit is supposed to be leading us?

The easy response is to suggest that, in effect, we are delivered from a particular lifestyle and culture in order to be transposed into another. Now that may seem easy and straightforward but it is a very difficult position to justify from Scripture. For the Bible would seem to imply that we are forgiven sinners called to continue living within the world, not attempting to escape from it. The reason is that we will be in the right place to encourage others to respond to the calling of divine love.

Rather than relaxing in self-satisfied contentment, we should always want others to discover for themselves that same saving faith which we have encountered in Jesus. Then they, too, can be the joyful recipients of the forgiveness, release and life-giving Holy Spirit that we have discovered. In other words, the blessings we have received are not only given to us for the purpose of our own comfort and enjoyment. They are given in order that we might share them with others. As Archbishop William Temple once observed, 'Christianity is the only society on earth which exists solely for the benefit of its non-members.'

The Authorised Version rendering of 2 Corinthians 6:17, in the language of 1611, reads, 'Come ye out from among them, and be ye separate, saith the Lord.' This too often became a catch-all licence excusing evangelical Christians from having to maintain any contact at all with the rest of humankind. We need always to be ready for the Holy Spirit to remind us that we have not been reborn in order to live separated lives, removed from the rest of the world. Instead he wants to work both in us and through us.

So we have not been brought into a self-centred relationship – a 'just me and Jesus together in a cosy huddle' kind of faith – but into one that is intended to be shared.

Contrary to the opinions of many, Christianity is an inclusive religion, not an exclusive one. It is because we have failed to grasp this truth that we have become submerged within our own sub-culture of 'Christian' activities, entertainments and programmes. One tragic result has been the emergence of the commonly held idea among non-Christians that the churches make little constructive contribution to human society and are therefore basically irrelevant.

The perceived irrelevance of the churches has largely emerged from the seeming inability of so many local evangelical churches to recognise any sense of corporate responsibility towards the rest of society. So often a new believer is given plenty of reasons to stay out of the world. Too often this appears to be a far preferable course of action to the alternative of getting involved in the local community in order to become a change-agent within it.

This was to prove to be a key issue for many who came from both my own and subsequent generations. It is often difficult for new converts, full of fresh zeal, enthusiasm and the Holy Spirit, to understand why it is that the faith they have now found should cause them to withdraw from the world rather than seek to transform it. It is hard for them to grasp why it is that the Jesus who is at work changing us from the inside could not perform the same miracle in the lives of their friends. The argument that a continued association with old non-Christian acquaintances might result in the compromise or even the destruction of their faith appears to contradict what they had so recently learned of the saving grace and power of Jesus.

Surely they had now received from the Holy Spirit a necessary anointing in order to overcome the assaults and rejection of this world rather than to be among those who cowered away in a corner and sought to avoid all contact with it? It is so that we might be equipped to live in our world and not seek to avoid it, to represent the cause of Christ to our world and not merely attempt to preserve our own sense of personal purity, that we have been anointed to live a new life.

Anointed for suffering

As the people of God, we have been promised two things – success and suffering. At first sight, these may seem mutually contradictory. Yet the success that we have been promised largely relates more to our future than to the present. Such an idea could scarcely be enthusiastically received in our modern world that is so dependent on notions of 'instant success'. So among many evangelical Christians, there has emerged a popular belief which maintains that the degree to which we are actively walking with God and serving him is indicated by the physical and material blessings that we have received. Put in its crudest form, the idea is that our openness to the Holy Spirit can be measured in terms of the condition of our physical health and the prosperity of our bank balance.

It is exceptionally difficult to pretend that such ideas fit in naturally with the example of one who denied himself the security of a home and possessed so little available cash that he took advantage of a conveniently floating fish in order to pay the tax bill for him and Simon Peter (Matt 8:20; 17:27). Jesus himself continually emphasised the demands of sacrificial discipleship and promised his disciples that they must always expect to suffer in his cause, so we certainly have no reason to anticipate an easier ride for ourselves in today's world.

The author Paul Billheimer once wrote words that have stayed with me as a spiritual warning through the years: 'The impression is current that to be saved and filled with the Spirit opens a charmed life entirely trouble-free, where all problems are instantaneously solved and where miracles never cease. According to some ... life is one hilarious roller-coaster picnic and lark. No one should ever get sick, or, if he does, he should be healed immediately by simple, effortless faith. If he needs money, all he has to do is ask God for it and the heavens open and down it pours. If anyone does not prosper and live affluently it is simply because he is not spiritually "on the ball"' (*Don't Waste Your Sorrows*, CLC, 1977).

These ideas have perniciously infiltrated themselves into the thoughts and lives of many Christians, often with disastrous consequences. For they cause us to focus our attention upon ourselves.

That is why Jesus introduced us to a concept that is far removed from so much contemporary thinking. He taught that we ourselves should be prepared to suffer for the sake of others. Nowhere is this more clearly taught than when he said, 'greater love has no-one than this, to lay down one's life for one's friends' (John 15:13, NIV). If this is the way that Jesus lived, then we should surely expect no less of ourselves. If we object that such unselfish living is an impossible goal for us to aim at, then the answer surely lies in the fact that this is one reason why the Holy Spirit has been given to us!

I don't know exactly how old Irma is. I would guess her to be in her fifties. Nor do I know the story of how she came to Jesus. I only know that she belongs to him, and the reason I know that to be true lies in her response to the tragic events of 13 January 2001. It is also because of how Irma lived and acted in the face of intense suffering that none of her neighbours could doubt the fact either.

It was around ten-thirty in the morning that the earthquake struck. Irma was in her house with two others from the local church. They were panic-stricken at the severity of the quake so they stood and held hands together believing in that instant that the end of the world had come. Then they heard the noise. It was like nothing that they had ever heard before. When the tremor stopped, and the three of them left Irma's house, they gazed around at what remained of the middle-class area of San Salvador in which they lived.

Looking up at the thickly wooded hillside that once overshadowed the dwellings, they realised with horror that about one-third of it was missing! The earthquake had dislodged the hillside and the trees had come crashing down on this peaceful and unsuspecting San Salvadorian suburb. Some trees had travelled a kilometre in distance before landing up in a kitchen or a lounge. What had immediately followed was a landslide with the dirt and scree crashing down to cover what remained of the houses. When the rescuers arrived, the area had become a vast communal graveyard, with survivors milling around in a state of total bewilderment. Then there were those such as Irma, whose houses stood on either side of the devastation, surveying the ravaged area in horror.

For the survivors, it was a moment of total confusion. For Irma, it was an opportunity, a chance to go and pray with those who stood there bewildered at all that had happened, and to offer what help and support she could. Many Christians had died, including at least one pastor. Two church buildings were condemned to be demolished. However, God's people were not thinking of themselves but of the sufferings of others. Pastor Saul had lost seven of his congregation, killed in the disaster. But he had survivors such as Irma who were ready and willing to get involved. So the distribution of food and clothing was swiftly arranged and Irma moved in, under an anointing from her Lord, to minister to the needs of those who had lost everything they possessed. The end-result of what was achieved in that and subsequent days will only be revealed in eternity.

We were not designed for an easy life. The Holy Spirit has come to make us into the hands and feet of Jesus. He himself has rightly been referred to as 'the tears of God'. This is scarcely inappropriate, for the way he chose to win us was one of 'suffering love'. He came to suffer and die in order that he might bring us to himself and he requires our own self-giving love in return (1 Cor 13:4–7). It is not through enjoying an easy life but by the way that we learn to deal with sorrow and pressure that God matures his people and teaches us how to share in the sufferings of others. It is through the discovery of our own Spirit-given capacity to endure tribulation that we will learn what it means to become more worthy of God's calling on our own lives (Heb 12:5–11).

The Apostle Paul clearly believed that suffering was to play a major role in the strategy of the Holy Spirit as he operated in our lives to prepare us for the glory that was to come (Rom 8:18; 2 Cor 4:17,18). That is the 'success' part of the arrangement because, as A W Tozer once remarked, we can afford to suffer here on earth because we are going to have eternity to enjoy ourselves. We have been called to share in the sufferings of Jesus because we have also been promised that one day we will begin an eternal triumphant reign as the bride of Christ. This is a reign on which there will be no time limits.

Anointed for blessing

It is certainly right to place emphasis on the fact that the Holy Spirit equips us to face up to and indeed conquer the tougher challenges that face us in life today. Too often this is a side of our faith that can be neglected. Some of us can be guilty of attempting to live in a naive triumphalism insisting that all things must always be automatically perfect for the people of God. As we have seen, nothing could be further from the truth.

However, it is possible to live in another extreme position. Simon Stylites, the early Christian ascetic, condemned himself to living for forty years on top of a fifty-foot pole. He did this because he viewed personal hardship as a basic part of the Christian life, and he believed that nothing could be more important than to keep himself untainted from the evils of a sin-sick world. The ancient Greek world saw suffering as a virtue in itself. That is not the Christian way, for we are called on to suffer in the here and now in order that we may extend God's kingdom. Suffering can never be regarded as an end in itself; God allows it because he wants to mature and bless his people.

Whether or not brother Stylites was right to live in the manner that he did is not for us to judge. What is important is to recognise that God longs to provide us with all that we need in order that we might live our lives for him. It is important to note that his estimate of what we need may not always agree with our own!

The 1990s witnessed a number of specific blessings being experienced by many of God's people. The ministry of the

'Kansas City prophets', the visits of John Wimber and the arrival of the 'Toronto blessing' all became much-discussed additional features on the charismatic evangelical landscape. Similarly, there were visits from Australian bishops and evangelical leaders, which created much excitement on the non-charismatic evangelical side of the equation. Yet because the latter addressed more cerebral issues, there was little controversy surrounding their visits. The same could not be said of more experiential emphases such as the 'Toronto blessing'.

It often seems that, as evangelical Christians, we love the opportunity to disagree with each other. In our fervour to defend our understanding of truth, we spend our time debating fiercely the merits of our case and the errors of those who disagree with us. Yet many of our brothers and sisters received a fresh release of the Holy Spirit in their lives. Many discovered refreshment at a time when their spiritual lives appeared to be arid and dry. I well remember one friend who, at that time, was facing up to a tough period in his life. He received prayer, and neither burst out in spontaneous laughter nor fell over backwards; he just rocked gently from side to side, seemingly cradled in the loving arms of Jesus. It was an incredibly comforting experience for him.

I will never forget the words of Bernard Levin when he wrote in *The Times* that he was not aware that laughing in church had yet been declared by ecclesiastical authorities to be a venal sin. Perhaps it takes the sane words of a Jewish commentator to persuade us to place our prejudices in perspective. For while we spend our time objecting to the spiritual experiences of one another our brothers and sisters around the world face suffering, persecution and death. Sometimes the indirect reason lies in our failure to come to their aid, through either our ignorance or our neglect.

It was this kind of mistaken zeal that, some years ago, made me write a book in angrier vein, entitled *With a Church like this, who needs Satan?* For when God wants to bless his people he follows no man-made prescription, and we should be ready and able to receive absolutely every blessing that he wants to shower upon us. What will prove more difficult will be to rejoice with others in what the Lord chooses to give to them but denies to us.

Now of course my saying this is not meant to imply that every aspect of what is trumpeted as the work of the Holy Spirit should be accepted as being 'of God'. Most evangelicals are rightly uncomfortable about some of the more extravagant edges of the charismatic movement. Prosperity theology, for example, distorts the biblical teaching about God blessing his people. Also an acceptance of the powerful work of the Holy Spirit today in blessing and equipping God's people need not imply that there needs to be an acceptance of everything the charismatic sub-culture puts on the counter. But none of this detracts from my main point, that 'the wind blows wherever it wishes' (John 3:8) and we must be careful not to quench the Spirit's fire. By all means let us 'put all things to the test' (1 Thess 5:21) and strongly emphasise that the Spirit is given to equip us for mission, not to gaze at our navels. But at the same time we need to recognise that God does not always work in conventional ways. Sometimes he speaks through donkeys (Num 22:22–35)!

Anointed to heal

Many years ago, I was conducting a coffee bar mission in a London suburb. While praying with a group of local Christians on the morning before the mission was due to begin, we were suddenly interrupted. A young nurse entered the room in tears. She had been longing to be involved in the mission. That morning her doctor had confirmed that she had perforated her eardrum. In a coffee bar atmosphere, she would be unable to hear well enough to share her faith.

I can't explain why I reacted so strongly, except that I knew this was not what God wanted. I urged the youth leader from a local Brethren assembly to stand with me and pray for the girl. Never before had I specifically prayed for healing for anyone. But she was healed! The youth leader was as surprised as I was, but he took things one step further – he married her!

Healing was so prominent in the ministry of Jesus that

many of us might wonder why Jesus spent so much valuable preaching time in this way. What made the practice of healing so very important in the ministry of Jesus?

Healing was an expression of the mind and will of God for humankind. Mark records the moment when 'A man suffering from a dreaded skin-disease came to Jesus, knelt down, and begged him for help. "If you want to," he said, "you can make me clean." Jesus was filled with pity, and reached out and touched him. "I want to," he answered. "Be clean!"' (Mark 1:40,41).

Healing was a sign of the compassion of Jesus. This is evidenced by the Greek word which Mark employs for 'pity'; this word, which is often used of the compassion of Jesus, means a love which flows from the human intestines. It comes from the very depths of a man or woman. This is no surface reaction or response; it is a heartfelt compassion, something which could genuinely be called a 'gut-level' love.

Healing was a fulfilment of prophecy: 'He did this to make what the prophet Isaiah had said come true, "He himself took our sickness and carried away our diseases"' (Matt 8:17).

Healing brings glory to God: 'He is blind so that God's power might be seen at work in him' (John 9:3).

Healing stimulates faith: 'Believe me when I say that I am in the Father and the Father is in me. If not, believe because of the things I do' (John 14:11).

It is amazing to see the changes that physical healing can introduce. Michael Cassidy tells this story.

'When I finally reached Chicago some weeks later, Lawrence Hammond greeted me warmly and told me his story. As I remember it at this time distance, it went something like this. He had been taken terribly ill with some kind of intestinal blockage and other problems. This landed him in hospital where his condition deteriorated horribly. His tummy had blown up to the size of a football and was grotesquely swollen.

The surgery decided upon did not apparently give much ground for hope. Having insisted on knowing his true condition, he had been told his chances were slender.

"I think they were mainly interested in me as a guinea pig for medical science," he said, laughing.

Anyway, he decided to call his Episcopal minister to come to his bedside to anoint him with oil and pray over him. This was two or three days before the operation.

He waited patiently, but desperation mounted as no minister appeared. Finally, on the day the operation was to take place, the new curate who had just come to their church arrived at his bedside in a state of jitters.

"I'm terribly sorry," he apologised, as he put his hat down on the bed. "The Rector is out of town and can't come so they asked me to come over. But I don't know what to do. They never taught us about healing at Seminary and I've never anointed with oil and I don't know what to do."

"My heart absolutely sank," Lawrence said to me. "I had set so much store by a visit from our minister as I knew he believed in healing. Now here I was with this poor young fellow, quite lost and at sea."

"Well," he went on, knowing he had me all goggle-eyed and transfixed, "I simply asked the curate if he believed God could heal, to which he replied in the affirmative. Then I asked him to lay hands on me and pray. The little fellow, almost ashen in colour, reached out his hands towards my bulging stomach. Then, as he touched me and before he could pray, it was as if a 3,000 volt electric current had gone through me. The curate got such a fright he rebounded from the bed and literally fell to the ground, knocking his hat flying off my bed as he did so. And there and then, the physical swelling of my stomach visibly subsided, like air coming out of a balloon or a soccer ball."

Lawrence's face glowed as he told the story. "So I pulled all the plastic tubes out of myself and leaped from my bed shouting, 'I've been healed, I've been healed!' By this time, the little curate was up off the ground and we sort of danced a jig round the ward. All this noise attracted the attention of the Jewish rabbi who was passing the ward. He had often seen me and knew the seriousness of my condition. As he perceived the spectacle, saw my normal-sized stomach and gathered what had happened, he rushed out of the door and down the passage, shouting, 'It's just like the Red Sea! It's just like the Red Sea!'"

So there they all were – the whooping patient, the dancing curate and the ecstatic rabbi – when several horrified nurses rushed in calling for order, calm and sanity.

"But he's been healed," beamed the curate.

"Yes, he has, he has, he has," bubbled the rabbi.

Anyway, the nurses, now joined by a doctor or two, finally got Lawrence back into bed.' (Michael Cassidy, *Bursting the Wineskins*).

Power – for Jesus, the early Church and indeed for Christians today – is no wild, irrational thing. Obviously we cannot control God, but to some extent we do have a certain control over whether or not God's power may work through us. There are conditions which need to be fulfilled in us if the Holy Spirit is to move freely through our lives.

Motives are important. As Simon the sorcerer discovered, money could not purchase God's power; it is not available just for anyone.

Prayer and fasting are sometimes the necessary preparation for God to empower his people (see Mark 9:29).

God's power is only available to his people and at his own initiative and intention (see Luke 10:9,21; Acts 5:12).

The glory and honour must go to God, not to those he has used as his servants (see Acts 3:9).

It is important to be grounded in the body of Christ, rightly related to Jesus, to one another and to our role and function within the body.

We must be careful not to presume that God's intention will be to heal on every single occasion. Though healing should normally be our expectation, we need to be careful not to encourage foolishness but to encourage faith. For that reason, we first seek to find God's will then act in obedience to that will, rather than our own desires, however good they may be!

I have discovered over the years that God's actions are spontaneous. He rarely chooses to fit into the well-worn pathways that I have devised for him. We operate in Jesus' name and only under his authority. Therefore we need to recognise that God does not respond to our own pet formulae. He tells us what to do, not vice versa.

There is real variety in what God does. Healing can be progressive or instantaneous, or God can call his people to endure suffering in order that he might fulfil his purposes. When the disciples tried to claim a monopoly on God's dealings, Jesus rebuked them. 'John spoke up, "Master, we saw a man driving out demons in your name, and we told him to stop, because he doesn't belong to our group." "Do not try to stop him," Jesus said to him and to the other disciples, "because whoever is not against you is for you."' (Luke 9:49,50).

We also need to recognise that frequently it may be God's will to heal through the wonderful work done by doctors and other medical practitioners. While sometimes God heals through direct supernatural interventions, at many other times he blesses the natural healing processes of the body, and the skilful, caring work of the medical profession.

One final point is that the Lord responds to faith rather than familiarity. When he went back to Nazareth, Jesus discovered that 'prophets are respected everywhere except in their own home town and by their relatives and their families.' For that reason 'he was not able to perform any miracles there, except that he placed his hands on a few sick people and healed them. He was greatly surprised, because the people did not have faith' (Mark 6:4–6).

Anointed to deliver

The strategy of Jesus was to take one life (his own) living outside Satan's stronghold and raise up thousands of others. This authority of his Holy Spirit is for Jesus alone to give. 'Listen! I have given you authority, so that you can walk on snakes and scorpions and overcome all the power of the Enemy, and nothing will hurt you' (Luke 10:19).

We could spend chapters just looking at this subject. So here are some brief guidelines.

Never go looking for demons. This is a ministry that should only be taken up reluctantly, when faced with situations of obvious need. Don't imagine the demonic where it doesn't exist; on the other hand, do listen to the voice of your spirit and the advice of others.

Distinguish carefully between levels of demonic activity – demonised, oppressed or, in very rare situations, possessed.

Be careful to distinguish between psychiatric or psychological disorder, which can be fostered by Satan, on the one hand and demonic activity on the other. Actually few of us are qualified to do this. It is always wise to seek the help of sympathetic Christian professionals whenever possible.

Don't act alone; always pray for wisdom; beware of being impetuous; and don't forget the law!

Don't lay hands on the demonised. Rebuke in Jesus' name and note that the vacuum must be filled, and damage healed, by the Holy Spirit (Luke 11:25).

Warn fellow Christians to avoid any association at all with areas of occultism; for example, horoscopes, psychic arts, the use of crystals, séances and astral projection.

Be careful not to give credit to Satan; don't get wrongly fascinated or interested, even under the guise of spiritual care. Exalt Jesus, dismiss the Devil!

It is important to avoid wasting time on those who have dabbled in the occult but have no desire to be freed from the results. There are six conditions for freedom:

Humility

Honesty

Confession of sin

Repentance

Forgiveness of all others

Calling on the name of the Lord

I hesitate even to mention this aspect of the Spirit's activity. We run the grave risk of demanding knowledge which is frankly unhelpful. The great number of books on Satan and all his works speaks volumes about the fascination that Satan can make the subject hold for the people of God. I far prefer the attitude expressed in a sentence from Canon Michael Green, to which I have already referred – I Believe in Satan's Downfall.

Anointed to bring good news to the poor

This anointing of the Holy Spirit is often ignored among the more spectacular demonstrations of his power! Yet the coming of Jesus as the Messiah was given convincing proof by the fact that his message of hope came to ordinary people. Jesus reserved some of his most devastating criticisms for the rich, and pointed out that the problems of wealth make it 'much harder for a rich person to enter the Kingdom of God than for a camel to go through the eye of a needle' (Mark 10:25). It is scarcely surprising that the disciples were 'completely amazed!' No longer were social privilege and income qualifications for spiritual superiority. The fact that 'Good News is preached to the poor' (Matt 11:5) was sent as a message by Jesus to John the Baptist to convince him, once and for all, that the Messiah had indeed arrived!

We cannot be satisfied with the facile suggestion that this emphasis was only necessary in Jesus' day. Today is his moment as well. The same needs still apply. About 800 million people, one-fifth of the human race, are destitute, lacking the basic necessities for survival.

We are all affected by global problems. TV and radio have removed our ignorance. Besieged by newsreel pictures of the poverty, starvation and death of thousands each day we can no longer claim that we are not aware of what is going on. Gross economic inequality is coupled to political oppression as people are denied fundamental human rights by totalitarian regimes of left and right alike.

In less extreme circumstances, racial and sexual discrimination create new problems that are often met by a stone wall of Christian apathy. Martin Luther King cried out in the face of such disinterest that, when we arrive at the judgement seat of Jesus Christ, we will have to confess not only the actions of the wicked but also 'the appalling apathy of the good'.

The declarations of God throughout history when he recognised and acted in cases of human suffering (Exod 3:7; Acts 7:34) culminated in Jesus' great sermon on the Mount of Olives. He urged his people to be 'salt for all mankind', but gave the stern warning that 'if salt loses its saltiness, there is no way to make it salty again. It has become worthless, so it is thrown out and people trample on it' (Matt 5:13). The last thirty-five years have witnessed a great awakening within evangelical Christianity to the social implications of the gospel. Organisations such as Tearfund, Care, Causeway, World Vision, the Shaftesbury Society and a whole host of others working either alongside or directly through the local church have helped to transform the evangelical landscape in the United Kingdom. This new awareness has graphically brought to life the significance of the words of Jesus, 'You are like light for the whole world ... so that they will see the good things you do and praise your Father in heaven' (Matt 5:14,16).

The Holy Spirit is given to be our helper, to encourage us to meet those needs that exist on our own doorstep.

The call comes to be distinctive both in what we say and in what we do, speaking God's word into situations and getting our hands dirty. The call to servant-hood, giving, love and prayer is the message of the Holy Spirit to us today in order that we might be for others 'the Word in working clothes'.

Loving our neighbour is not something that we can leave to a welfare state! It is as we visit others, as we get involved in the life of the community, that we spread the true message of Jesus to the poor.

As we face the needs of those who suffer from poverty, discrimination and hurt or those who lack water, health care, education or employment, the Holy Spirit issues specific calls on our lives. The elderly, unemployed, sick, disabled, low wage earners, those living in overcrowded conditions, those in ethnic minority groups and many others all need to see the demonstration of the love of Jesus. Only then can the church be seen as no longer an impersonal, authoritarian institution, but a caring, helping body of real people.

David Watson was one of the most well-loved and best-known leaders in the early days of the charismatic movement. He commented from his experience as an Anglican vicar that 'evangelism and social action are like the two blades of a pair of scissors: if you have one without the other, you lose your cutting edge.'

A simple illustration can be found in the way several churches have faced the problem of the mounting unemployment among young people. Instead of just observing the situation, churches have adapted their premises as drop-in centres for the unemployed. Here training can be given in job application and interview procedures. Community enterprise projects and job creation schemes under Christian supervision have been developed. An informal atmosphere provides opportunities for Christian and non-Christian unemployed to relax and work together. A bonus has been the way that this opportunity for Christian witness removes many of the debilitating effects of the feeling of uselessness that many young Christians face.

God called his people Israel to be unique. He called them to be an example of social concern. They were to be committed to the poor, needy, widowed and orphaned: ruled by justice, peace and love, with no slaves or elaborate social hierarchy. For our part, do we give to the poor, the elderly or the disadvantaged? Furthermore, we need to ask whether our generosity stops at home, or whether it extends overseas as well. Tearfund and other similar agencies do provide the evangelical churches of Britain with a wonderful opportunity to demonstrate that we still believe we are only a part of the church universal. When our brothers and sisters in other parts of the world need our help, we should be happy to demonstrate what it means to belong to another Kingdom.

Or are we more concerned about 'designer labels'? Do we flaunt our wealth with large houses, new cars and the latest fashion trend? Are we guilty of judging people by external appearances? Do we enjoy controlling others, even seeking power, or do we practise 'downward mobility' and allow our lives to focus on love and concern for those who have fewer material possessions than we have ourselves? The problem is that some of us will be tempted to turn off at this point. We readily feel 'got at' or tempted to react to the idea that we are being pushed into a 'guilt-trip'. Yet the real issue does not lie in condemning ourselves for the good things that God has provided for us. It is not a question of what we possess but rather of what we are prepared to give to others.

For far too long, we have been prepared to give credence to the idea that the anointing is a matter of what we can receive for us. It is not. The anointing that God provides for his servants is fundamentally about what the Holy Spirit is doing in our lives not for us ourselves but in order that we might give of the very best for others.

Too often we have been content to view the Holy Spirit as just a useful adjunct to our own lives. In John's Gospel, the Holy Spirit is referred to in various translations as Advocate, Counsellor, Helper and Comforter. In fact, he is a combination of all four: an advocate to plead our case, a counsellor to guide and a helper to assist us in all those things that we can never do alone. But a comforter?

The picture of comfort which the translators of the seventeenth century Authorised Version envisaged was not of a sympathetic ear! The Bayeux Tapestry of the Norman victory in 1066 depicts one of Duke William's supporters prodding into battle a Norman soldier, a reluctant hero, with the point of a spear in his rear. Underneath this picture is the comment that King William 'comforteth his soldiers'!

The Holy Spirit is the one who mobilises us for battle. His anointing is for the healing of the brokenhearted, the defeat of the enemy and the proclamation of the gospel to the poor.

Chapter 6

How God guides

'A baby rabbit fell into a quarry's mixing machine yesterday and came out in the middle of a concrete block. But the rabbit still had the strength to dig its way free before the block set.

The tiny creature was scooped up with thirty tons of sand, then swirled and pounded through the complete mixing process... With the thirty tons of sand, it was dropped into a weighing hopper and carried by conveyor to an overhead mixer where it was whirled around with gallons of water.

From there the rabbit was swept to a machine, which hammers wet concrete into blocks, by pressure of 100 pounds per square inch. The rabbit was encased in a block eighteen inches long, nine inches high and six inches thick. Finally the blocks were ejected on to the floor to dry and the dazed rabbit clawed itself free! We cleaned him up, dried him by the electric fire, then he hopped away!'
(The Best of Shrdlu).

Many see their own lives reflected in just this kind of picture. A poor innocent caught in the vast machine of life, only just managing to escape. For the Christian, such a picture completely fails to capture the truth. In giving our lives to Jesus Christ, we have placed ourselves under his control. But why then do so many accidents of life occur which, clearly to our minds, could not be in the will and purpose of God for us? The answer clearly lies within the kind of redirection which the living God longs to provide for our lives.

I remember the days when my oldest son Kris was only six years old. Whenever I came home from being away for a few days, I found that I could suggest just about any activity to him, and he would happily agree, demonstrating an unusual degree of compliance. So we could go and take the dog for a walk, have a game of football together or go shopping in town – pretty well any suggestion would receive the one word reply, 'Great.' He was so pleased to have his daddy home that he seemed happy to respond to pretty well any suggestion that I might choose to make. He just wanted to be with Dad and he trusted my judgement as to what we should do together.

Later in life, when teenage years arrived, things did indeed begin to change. He became even more aware of the fact that he possessed a will of his own. He would express his own desires and if they conflicted with mine, a meaningful dialogue would duly ensue! If disagreement continued, I faced a serious choice. Either I had to attempt to impose my will or leave it up to my son and trust that either he or I would learn lessons from our mistakes. Much would always depend on just how serious we each considered the issue.

However, because I am not God, the analogy naturally breaks down. Kris's course of action may actually have proved to be better than what I proposed. With a loving God who is totally committed to us, that possibility cannot exist. He loves us so much that he can only desire the best for his people.

God does not push his guidance on to us. He is no arbitrary deity just trying to get his own way, but he longs to bring fulfilment to our lives. He looks for a people who will trust him as their Creator to bring the best for them, a people whom he can involve in the unfolding of his purposes in their nation and his world. That is why he does not leave us blindly to pursue our own pathway but offers himself as the highest quality of guide that this world has ever known.

Nevertheless, God does still leave it in our hands to demon-strate through our obedience the right and necessary response to the guide he has provided for us. His guidance is up to us to be sensitive to and respond to – he has not chosen to make us a part of some rigid, automatic process. He has never been content just to wind us up as if we were mere clockwork robots, pre-programmed to conform to his will for our lives. In Psalm 32:8,9, for example, a clear promise to guide us is accompanied by an equally clear instruction to be sensitive to his leading: 'The Lord says, "I will teach you the way you should go; I will instruct you and advise you. Don't be stupid like a horse or mule which must be controlled with a bit and bridle to make it submit".' Basically, God waits to know whether we wish to listen to the voice of his Spirit as he seeks to offer direction for our lives or whether we are stubbornly determined to stick with the folly of only wanting to persist with following our own inclinations.

Parting gift

So how then can we hear and understand what God wants us to do? It is so difficult to be sure when God is speaking to us; all too often we are left wondering if this was God or just our own imagination?

Shortly before he died, Jesus made what some have seen as his last will and testament. He bequeathed his body to Joseph of Arimathea, his clothes to the soldiers who were killing him, his mother to his beloved disciple John and his spirit to his Father, but he left to his disciples a very special promise in the words: 'Peace is what I leave with you; it is my own peace that I give you' (John 14:27). He appointed no executor to ensure that the provisions of his will were fulfilled, instead it was after his resurrection that he personally visited them in order to ensure that they received his parting gift. Without creating any damage, he broke through a wall in order to greet them with the words, 'Peace be with you' (John 20:19).

The parting gift of Jesus to his followers was a peace which the world can never provide, which only the Holy Spirit can give. Paul comments about this peace in his letter to the Colossians: 'The peace that Christ gives is to guide you in the decisions you make' (Col 3:15).

Jesus emphasised this same truth when he made a marvellous promise to his followers; he pledged that we would not be left as orphans in a pagan world. Instead the Holy Spirit would come to us: 'he will lead you into all the truth' (John 16:13). In other words, the Holy Spirit has come to direct our lives, and the peace of God rules in our hearts to confirm that guidance.

Listening for beginners

'How can I be sure?'

If I had a pound for every time I've been asked that question, I'd be a wealthy man! God's Spirit has so many ways of guiding us, some dramatic, some gentle – but only very rarely anything as dramatic as writing on the wall.

As we look at the variety of ways in which God leads his people, we will recognise one common factor. It is within the intimacy of a deep, personal relationship with Jesus through the Holy Spirit that we find he can direct our lives. It is only as we surrender our lives in an ever-deepening commitment to Jesus and listen for the voice of his Spirit that his purposes for us as individuals today become clear.

In Scripture: here we are on completely safe ground. God never changes his mind or contradicts his Word. As the Psalmist has said, 'Your word is a lamp to guide me and a light for my path' (Ps 119:105). Following Jesus must always involve obedience to the Spirit's Word in Scripture. Any claim to guidance which goes against the clear teaching of the Bible must be immediately rejected. If we think we are being led to have sex outside of marriage, for example, then the guidance does not come from the Spirit! Any other way in which we believe God may be guiding us must always be tested by the teaching of Scripture.

Practically, there are at least three ways in which we need to approach the Bible. First, it is crucial that we try to read as much of it as possible so that we can get a sense of the 'big picture', God's wonderful plan of salvation, in all its key stages. Secondly, the more we can study the Bible, trying to understand what the original readers would have made of its message, the better we will be able to discern the underlying principles which the Holy Spirit can help us to apply in our very different cultural contexts. Thirdly, we need to meditate on the Bible, allowing its life-giving words to soak into our very being. Christians have found from experience that nothing builds us up more or helps us to be more open to God than regularly feeding on his Word. These three ways of approaching the Bible can be summarised as reading it as if it were a newspaper, a textbook and a love letter. All three are important, and they complement each other. As we ask the Lord to speak to us as we read, study and meditate on the Bible we will find both that we get to know him better and that he guides us in the details of our daily lives.

In circumstances: this is perhaps the most common manner in which Christians receive guidance. Yet it is notoriously unreliable.

Of course, the Holy Spirit can and does guide through circumstances but we must be very careful to be certain that it is his hand that lies behind each situation. It is here that we need the peace of God to act as the signal to our hearts.

Several years ago Ruth and I found ourselves in a real quandary while we were engaged in seeking direction for the future. Every circumstance in this particular situation seemed to point forward in a particular direction for the two of us. Yet Ruth felt a real absence of peace, a sense of disquiet fermenting within her. We therefore became unusually cautious. We proceeded very slowly indeed, believing that God would either clearly confirm this check or dismiss it. Not many days afterwards, the Lord brought his word to us through a close friend that we should take the matter no further. This later proved to have been the right decision. I might struggle as a man to acknowledge that my wife was right but I have observed over the years that the woman is often more sensitive and open to divine direction than the man.

In following: God's intention has never been just to prod us from behind. His call to disciples is always to 'follow me'. In other words, God's Spirit will always travel ahead of us, preparing the ground so that we can follow in his footsteps. As we see how God is working in a particular situation, we need to fit in with that and be sensitive to the Spirit's direction. If we choose not to follow God's leading, we soon lose that sense of peace. Although we cannot just fall in and out of the Spirit of God, we can obey or disobey. As the late Denis Clark wisely used to comment about driving on motorways within the law of the land, 'Up to seventy miles per hour the Lord is with you, over that you're on your own!'

In people: here again we must proceed with caution. God's Spirit can lead us through others but only within the confines of his revealed word in Scripture. Paul himself knew how to reject advice as well as receive it. 'By the power of the Spirit, they told Paul not to go to Jerusalem. But when our time with them was over, we left and went on our way' (Acts 21:4,5). However well-intentioned the advice, we must always assess it and test its value before the Lord even if it is not against scriptural teaching (1 Thess 5:19–21).

Often when God intends something for us he will reveal it to more than one person – and confirm it for us as well!

A few years ago, I returned from a fortnight of mission in Sussex to be greeted by my wife with the words, 'Darling, I think you ought to go to Israel.' In all our years of marriage, she had never made such a suggestion. There was desire at work here, because Ruth was well aware of the fact that for many years I had wanted to visit the land of Israel, but although human reasons for the idea existed, she firmly believed that this idea had originated within the will of God.

Consequently she had contacted a friend of ours who frequently took parties to Israel but he had nothing planned at that time. She also discovered that the cost would have been completely prohibitive for us. We were both in the process of dismissing the idea when, some three days later, a friend who had known nothing of this called me. His words came right out of the blue when he announced that he had felt firmly convinced that the Lord wanted him to make a visit to Israel in three weeks' time. He had never been to that country before but sensed that the Lord had placed this conviction so firmly on his heart that he was not at liberty to ignore it! Having purchased his ticket, he had felt equally constrained to buy one for me as well. He also knew nothing of my secret desires to go there. The next day, I discovered my engagements for the relevant week had been suddenly cancelled. When God intends something for his people, he brings it all together!

In dreams: God does not try to hide his will from us. If he recognises that for the best of reasons we are missing his way for us, the Lord will sometimes intervene while we are asleep. Paul experienced this when 'that night Paul had a vision in which he saw a Macedonian standing and begging him, "Come over to Macedonia and help us!"' (Acts 16:9). Immediately he responded to God's call. We need to be careful to judge our dreams and visions correctly. Sometimes they can be divinely or demonically inspired, although the latter is unusual for Christians. What is more likely is that they may be mere fantasy or the result of eating too much pizza the night before! We should not jump too quickly to the conclusion that God is telling us to do something, especially if we have not been living in a close relationship with him. But sometimes we may have a sense that a dream is significant, and in this case it is good to share it with other Christians whom we trust.

In listening: there are so many ways in which we hear God. Through inspired speech, word of knowledge, word of wisdom or prophecy, through the sense of agreement with others or through the gentle nudge of direction from the Spirit. (This will be experienced as a quiet inner conviction – but we must be careful, for our own active imagination may well mislead.) All these ways of hearing God require testing. The best context for receiving revelation lies in the practice of the early church illustrated at Antioch where they gathered to fast and pray. In that context, the Holy Spirit spoke (Acts 13:2).

Sometimes Christians become very worried about guidance. They wonder if they have missed out somewhere. God does not want that. It is right for us to look for God's way but not to be worried and concerned. God wants us to experience joy in finding his way - and we are more likely to do that if we get on with living where we are and working on our relationship with Jesus. Then we'll be ready to hear God's voice when he wants us to move. If we start worrying about the next step too soon we'll start imagining all sorts of things that aren't really there. Jesus reminds us, '... be concerned above everything else with the Kingdom of God and with what he requires of you ... do not worry about tomorrow' (Matt 6:33,34).

It is all too easy to become over-concerned with the detail of God's plan for our lives and lose sight of his overall purpose. The wonderful truth is that God's main purpose for us is to make us like Jesus. 'Those whom God had already chosen, he also set apart to become like his Son ...' (Rom 8:29).

God never wants us to miss his way for us. Paul discovered that when he and his companions wanted to go to Bithynia against the will of God, 'the Spirit of Jesus did not allow them' (Acts 16:7). This is more than just an indication of his loving commitment to us. He longs that we will not go astray. However well-intentioned we may be, our mistaken notions of what would be right for us may often mean that the Holy Spirit has to take action in order to prevent us from wandering off in the wrong direction.

Now God may well fence us in by creating major obstacles to our wandering out of line, but these are actions of love to prevent us hurting ourselves too deeply or damaging our lives too much. This is vividly illustrated by Hosea's relationship with his unfaithful wife Gomer, which God uses to show in picture form how his people Israel have lived in relationship to the Lord. 'So I am going to fence her in with thorn bushes and build a wall to block her way. She will run after her lovers but will not catch them. She will look for them but will not find them. Then she will say, "I am going back to my first husband – I was better off then than I am now"' (Hos 2:6,7).

Ultimately it is our obedience to his revealed will and our response to the trials life inevitably throws up which is crucial. Through all the decisions of life, big and small, we can have the wonderful privilege of deepening our relationship with the Lord as we ask for his direction and commit everything to him.

Jesus is at work within our lives. Through his Holy Spirit he is endeavouring to teach us the lessons of what it means to live in God's world and how we can live in it God's way.

Jesus told his disciples that they would actually be better off without him: 'I am telling you the truth: it is better for you that I go away, because if I do not go, the Helper will not come to you' (John 16:7). Impossible as it may seem for all of us who would love to have walked and talked by Galilee with Jesus, he said that we are in a superior position! Because he has come, we do not have God walking alongside us but actually know him living within us!

No Christian can ever be regarded as being at the mercy of a vicious, fallen world. We are far from helpless victims. Unlike the rabbit trapped by forces beyond its control and fortunate to escape, we have been provided with the finest guide through life this world has ever known – the Holy Spirit – God himself.

Chapter 7

Enemy at work

She was so excited – really thrilled. Victory had been so sudden and totally overwhelming. God had just intervened and it had all been so unexpected. She had always wanted God to use her life in a major way. Now it had all happened and the details were unimportant.

Then she was alone and very tired. Somehow things could never be quite the same again. The moment of highest achievement had come but it had also gone again. Perhaps it is inevitable that at that moment temptation struck, just when she least expected it. Sometimes we just plain forget that we have an enemy at work – and he is against us.

Elijah would have sympathised. He went through the same kind of routine until he was rescued by the still, quiet voice of the Spirit of God. After his moment of greatest triumph at the top of Mount Carmel, he found himself running for his life in order to escape the clutches of an evil queen. So unaware was he of the potential for intervention on the part of the all-powerful Holy Spirit that he even contemplated suicide.

There is nothing unusual in this particular sequence of events. Jesus has had thirty years in total obscurity. He emerges from Nazareth, just about the most unlikely place imaginable! He is publicly baptised by John and at that moment God the Father speaks from heaven to endorse his Son. At that point of triumph, vindicated before his fellow-countrymen, the Holy Spirit drives Jesus into the desert in order that he might be tempted by the enemy.

It is easy to ask, 'Why?' Is this the way God repays faithful service? Yes, in a way, it is. After all, Jesus warned us that if we are faithful in small things, we will be trusted with bigger matters. So often we view temptation as entirely a negative factor. Yet on many occasions, that conclusion would be far from the truth. Satan will always view temptation as his moment to score yet time and again, God is simply allowing him to over-stretch himself so that our moment of potential tragedy might be reversed and turned into one of triumph. At these times, Satan chooses the moment when he believes we are most vulnerable and God uses that period when we are tested to strengthen and equip us for our Christian life and witness – checkmate!

Tired, hungry and alone, Jesus faced Satan himself. But the Holy Spirit had placed him in that position for a reason!

The Desert

The three years of ministry which lay ahead of Jesus were to be the most crucial period in the history of humankind. After this life, the world would never be the same again. It was the task of the Holy Spirit to be the teacher of Jesus, to prepare him for his life of ministry. In exactly the same way, Jesus promised, 'the Counsellor, the Holy Spirit, whom the Father will send in my name, will teach you all things' (John 14:26, NIV). However, a teacher needs a classroom so the Holy Spirit sent Jesus to his traditional training ground – the desert.

The road to spiritual maturity is not an easy one. Frequently it lies through what many have termed a 'wilderness experience' and at times when we are tired, alone and feeling that we have lost touch with God, Satan sees and seizes his opportunity.

It was in the physical wilderness that the Holy Spirit taught Israel. The desert was the training-ground for John the Baptist who fulfilled his training so well that Jesus testified of John, 'I tell you, among those born of women, there is no one greater than John' (Luke 7:28, NIV).

First of all, Jesus fasted to prepare himself for the conflict for, as he was later to emphasise, some battles can never be won without just that kind of preparation. For the Christian life has never been a glib exercise in 'easy-believism', but rather it has always been a clear-cut struggle with no less an opponent than the enemy of our souls, Satan himself.

In this serious exercise of spiritual warfare, it is of vital importance to notice that we are engaged in a series of conflicts not merely with wrong habits or ideas but with an actual and personal enemy who represents spiritual reality at its very worst.

For this reason, Satan can never be simply dismissed as an irrational fear or as a joke. Yet although this enemy is to be treated with respect, he is not to be regarded as all-powerful or to be treated with dread. Scripture is quite insistent that while there is a personal devil, he is not comparable for a single moment with God himself. Satan is a strong and persuasive opponent but he is one who has already been conquered. For the victory over this enemy has already been won on our behalf therefore we do not need to be afraid.

Throughout the centuries of the life of the Christian Church, there has always been that select bunch of individuals who have actually known that this was true! They did not let the reality of it languish in theory but simply put it into practice. During the Reformation in the sixteenth century, Martin Luther sensed that he was undergoing a close encounter with Satan himself and ended up throwing an ink pot at his old enemy!

The twentieth century witnessed the same kind of spiritual confidence at work when that great Pentecostal evangelist and church-planter Smith Wigglesworth was disturbed from his sleep at around four o'clock one morning, and woke up to find Satan standing at the foot of his bed. Despite being both startled and surprised, he managed to make a truly Biblical and theologically correct response. He simply said, 'Oh, it's you,' and turned over and went to sleep again.

The reason that he could do this rested in the simple fact that he had realised that when we have inherited a new life in Christ Jesus, we really do have nothing to be afraid of, except to obey our Father God and seek to do his will. This point is made no fewer than 366 times in the Bible, when we are repeatedly given the instruction and reassurance, 'Don't be afraid.' In other words, we have nothing to fear.

So why are these comforting words repeated so often? Once for every day of the year and an extra one for leap years. The need to go on and on making the point comes from the fact that it is absolutely essential for each one of us to take hold of this one truth.

The reason for this repetition is undoubtedly because we tend to be slow learners. Most of us do not learn these truths automatically. We regard a 'desert experience' as something negative, a period where we just have to concentrate on survival but, as it was for Jesus, so often it is God's schoolroom in which to prepare us for all that lies ahead. It is not when life is easy but rather when we are going through difficult times that God will often choose to speak directly to us. It is not in the spiritual 'highs' but while we are enduring an arid wilderness experience that God demonstrates to us the reality of the fact that his victory over the enemy is a basic part of our spiritual birthright.

If Satan had won his conflict with Jesus in the wilderness, then God's plan of redemption would have failed. This was not to be the case because, led by the Spirit, Jesus was ready. Once the conflict was successfully over, angels were ready to assist the Son of God to make a swift and total recovery. In boxing terms, it had been victory by a first round knockout, but the gymnasium in which to prepare for the fight, as well as the arena itself, was the desert.

The Devil

Some Christians manage to live most of their spiritual lives in blissful ignorance of the Devil's very existence. This is because they never trouble him so he rarely bothers them!

The very idea of a personal Devil is enough to cause many to break out into guffaws of laughter. Yet these very same folks find nothing strange in accepting the necessity for avoiding ladders, touching wood or even 'kissing the blarney stone'. Notions of devouring alien monsters, ancient curses which have retained their virulent potency and even of extra-terrestrial beings enjoying a brief excursion to planet Earth are nowadays all regarded as perfectly possible. But the concept of a personalised demonic architect of evil – Satan himself? No way! It seems to me that as human beings we are becoming very selective in our acceptance of the supernatural. We appear to be quite happy with whatever falls within our comfort-zones or can provide us with further entertainment value. To contemplate the existence of a Devil who has his own personality and possesses the power to invade ours as well is, for most people, quite out of the question.

The modern mind finds it almost impossible to cope with the notion that Satan could be real. It all seemed to be outside the realm of possibility. This is easy to understand when we consider that the very idea of Satan conflicts with the basic presuppositions of our contemporary world-view.

We may ask, 'Why is this?' The answers are quite straightforward: How can a materialistic world accept the existence of a non-material being?

How can a rational world accept the existence of a force that is only acknowledged by what is perceived as a lunatic fringe of Satanists or devil-worshippers?

How can the 'spiritual' be allowed to intrude into a world that is reluctant even to talk about that dimension except where it is reduced to the level of 'the force' in Star Wars?

How can 'evil' be spoken of when we reject its existence?

The simple fact remains that the very idea of Satan does not agree with a twenty-first century mindset. The age of hedonism is alive and well and living among us. Our postmodern world has decided that everything is there to be enjoyed. We may acknowledge a little inconsistency in maintaining a world of ideas in which a fascination with the paranormal is allowed to exist alongside a rejection of all that cannot be appreciated through our five senses. But we hate ever to admit the possibility that we could be wrong, so everything interesting is let in while ideas of God and Satan, good and evil, are left firmly locked out.

C S Lewis once perceptively observed: 'There are two equal and opposite errors into which our race can fall about devils. One is to disbelieve their existence. The other is to believe and to feel an unhealthy interest in them. They themselves are equally pleased by both errors and hail a materialist or a magician with the same delight' (*The Screwtape Letters*, Collins, 1942).

Once we begin to show an interest in being totally committed to God and living in the power of the Holy Spirit, then that is the moment for Satan to start to worry! For he fears the conflict and exposure that may result when he is exposed to the light. He far prefers the darkness and appreciates the immunity and protection that it gives him. He hates to be challenged because he fears those who might wake up and stand against him. The plain and simple fact is that he is really a coward at heart.

These statements may sound surprising, but the reason for them is best understood when we begin to recognise who he really is, and contrast his very limited power and personality with that of the Holy Spirit.

He is a defeated opponent. In the first place, Satan was only a created being. He possesses more of the attributes of humankind than of the divine for he employs violence in order to achieve his objectives and is a liar, a deceiver, and one who gets it wrong! Nowhere is this more clearly illustrated than on the occasion that the devil stared defeat in the face – and he panicked. It took place two thousand years ago when Satan observed a situation which he had always dreaded could happen. One thing he could not tolerate was God's Son bringing salvation and freedom to ordinary men and women. He set out to frustrate God's purposes but instead he ended up doing the very things that were necessary to accomplish them!

Satan engineered his vassals to get Jesus nailed onto a cross. Looking at a crucified Jesus, he was convinced that he had rid himself of the one man who had dared to live to the full in the power and authority of the Holy Spirit. Three days later, God, through that same Holy Spirit, took Jesus out of the grave and restored him to his side. The created world looked on in amazement. Whoever heard of a God who would suffer, let alone die, for his own creation? Within days, there were one hundred and twenty, then three thousand, then a completely uncountable number whose lives were filled with the Holy Spirit and were consequently seeking to live in the way that God had always intended for them.

Satan is the victim of a major disadvantage. His pride makes him try to compete in the wrong league. He is only a created being who was expelled from heaven for seeking to oppose God. As such he can never aspire to be a true opponent of the

Holy Spirit. What is more Satan knows it – and fears! Throughout the centuries there have been many outstanding Christians who have recognised this fact. It is only because there are so many of us who have either ignored or rejected this truth that the Devil has got away with as much as he has!

Satan is limited in time and space. He can only be in one place at a time. The Holy Spirit, on the other hand, can be everywhere at the same instant. Satan is terribly limited and has to employ an army of demon spirits to move at his command. For this reason, one is very unlikely to have a personal encounter with Satan. His activities are both temporary and localised. What a contrast to the Holy Spirit who comes to live inside the people of God all day long!

In one sense we ought to rejoice on the exceptionally rare occurrence when Satan might come to trouble us in person as it would mean that we were saving all our brothers and sisters throughout the world from having a problem!

Satan's bitterness and anger are so fierce that he has engaged in violent actions against those who have given the direction of their lives to the Holy Spirit. The response that the Devil wants to make towards Spirit-filled lives resembles the attitude displayed in a warning sign outside a Beverly Hills house: 'Warning – Trespassers will be shot. Survivors will be prosecuted.'

Recognising that this lies beyond his powers, Satan has instead chosen to concentrate on trying to get us hung up on inessentials, spending hours arguing about issues that have no direct impact on how we live rather than getting on with the business of serving Jesus in his world. Satan tried through every means at his disposal to make us afraid of the Holy Spirit, leading us to see him as a cause of division rather than unity. The Devil's strategy was brilliantly simple. He tried to make us feel either arrogant because of some experience we had or inferior because we lacked it!

How easy it is to fall for Satan's deception! Our spiritual insecurities can make us far too easy a prey for him. We seem to be so afraid that others will be ahead of us in the race, that instead of rejoicing at the way God leads them, we insist that they come back to join us on our own spiritual pathway.

In the New Testament, the Greek word for Satan – *satanas* – only rarely carries the meaning of being our 'opponent'. Now we know that Jesus is the victor. It is by his Spirit that we triumph over Satan. This is why he so rarely dares to stand against us. More frequently the word means 'accuser'. Satan creeps up behind us, whispering words to create doubt as to whether God could ever do anything with people like us. Once he has managed to make us begin to question the power and activity of the Holy Spirit in our lives, it is a short distance to making us doubt whether or not we really are Christian. After all, if the Spirit is God, he should be able to deal with us or are we only kidding ourselves?

There can be no cause to enquire as to where such reactions come from We are left with an inescapable conclusion – an enemy has done this!

The Decisive Factor

Sadly, many of us are strangely silent when it comes to issues relating to the reality of the Holy Spirit. As has already been pointed out, it is a sad fact that throughout the history of the Church theologians have often seemed less confident in talking about God the Holy Spirit than about the Father or the Son. Controversy has often dogged the activities of the Holy Spirit. Continually people have objected to claims of his activity by responding that God cannot work in this way or the other. Certainly we feel safer with the activities of God the Father, revealed in creation, or the Son as we see him in Jesus. The dominant activities of the Holy Spirit lie in the here and now and that appears to be far more dangerous. We feel safer looking into the past than in experiencing God's power in our lives in the present!

Jesus promised his disciples that they would not have to struggle on in their own strength. 'I will not leave you as orphans; I will come to you' (John 14:18, NIV). So the major difficulty that confronts us is that each and every one of us is incapable of living the life of God without the power of the Holy Spirit, 'Even though the desire to do good is in me, I am not able to do it' (Rom 7:18). But the amazing news is that God has not abandoned us to this problem. He has not left us to struggle on somehow trying to survive alone. Rather than being neglected orphans, we are the proud possessors of God's Holy Spirit. It is incredibly easy to forget that this Spirit is the Holy Spirit. He expects us to be holy, too, and works in our lives to bring that about but that will inevitably bring down upon us the direct opposition of Satan himself.

Jesus could only face life on earth in opposition to the will of Satan through the Holy Spirit. As soon as Jesus was baptised, the Holy Spirit filled him. 'He saw the Spirit of God coming down like a dove and alighting on him' (Matt 3:16). F B Meyer, that great evangelical preacher of the early years of the twentieth century, reminded his hearers that they should 'never forget that our Lord's ministry was not in the power of the second Person of the blessed Trinity but in the power of the third Person.' Similarly, in a new century, we need to remember that same lesson.

The Dilemma stones into bread

Of the three direct challenges which he received from Satan, this must have seemed the most straightforward. Scripture states simply that after a forty day fast, 'he was hungry' (Luke 4:2). Most of us would have been!

Satan is a specialist in the field of easy answers and he offers a simple solution because he knows that if Jesus simply turns these stones into bread, then he will have misused his divine power by employing it to simply alleviate his own hunger.

A few weeks later, Jesus was to feed crowds of four and five thousand with a few loaves and fish. All he had to do was to advance God's own basic strategy by a matter of weeks and Jesus could satisfy his own physical needs. Time and again, it is at this level of self-interest that Satan will strike. He will offer anything to keep us complacent and self-indulgent. Satisfy yourself, enjoy your meetings, books, conferences, records and friends – just don't exercise spiritual concern for others. Save it for yourself. Don't waste your time on the needs of those around you but concentrate on number one. One could even suggest that the temptation would include the desire to satisfy our own spiritual needs, even our own desire to be holy. Anything seems to be acceptable to Satan if it means that we are content to leave him alone within his own dominion.

Now this is directly opposed to those concerns which are prompted by the Holy Spirit in our own lives. He wants to mobilise us to reach out from our spiritual ghettos into a dying world. Satan, on the other hand, desperately wants to keep us fat, self-interested, relatively content and at home!

That is why the Devil is not overly concerned about our correct attitudes in abstaining from certain sinful appetites. Of course these are important. Personal holiness must always be a major issue for Christian believers but never at the expense of ignoring social injustice and the pain of others in our world. This is a subject on which the Bible has even more to say and we neglect one truth at the expense of the other at our personal peril. While we concentrate on avoiding relatively minor pitfalls, Satan is hammering home on major issues. Too often the result is a sense of spiritual self-indulgence as we live in a world that is rarely able to listen to the message of Jesus because too often we, as his followers, are busy employing the majority of our talents for our own spiritual benefit.

The Danger - cheap gains

Satan's offers of help are usually attractive and this second one was no exception for Jesus. He is offered his divine legacy of the kingdoms of the world but without the pain of the cross. All he had to do was to worship his enemy.

The temptation is to follow an easy pathway. Satan's gift to Jesus would only, at best, have been temporary. God's legacy to his obedient Son is going to be eternal. In exactly the same way, we face the choice between our own short-lived ambitions or the direction which God has prepared for our lives.

Such commitment will seem strange to others in society. I can well remember the occasion when God chose to tell one of the leaders in a local church to sell his private house and purchase a council dwelling on a neighbouring estate where church contacts and influence were few and far between. The corporation found it difficult to understand but following the living God can usually be expected to be neither easy nor cheap. As Christians, we are faced with a simple choice. It lies between bowing the knee to Satan for short-term gain or looking to Jesus for an eternal inheritance.

This may involve the inconvenience of moving house to live in a less desirable area. It can mean changing jobs or even facing suffering, persecution or both! But as A W Tozer aptly put it, 'We can afford to suffer here on earth, we will have eternity to enjoy ourselves.' The Holy Spirit has been given to lead us into truth. It is to his direction that we must turn if we are to follow God's way for our lives because we can never succeed on our own. Having done that, we then need to get on with it!

The Deception   destroy yourself!

Satan knows his Bible so is good at quoting it out of context. He offers Jesus a shortcut to avoid the cross, an easy route leading to instant popularity. Throw yourself down – God's angels will catch you! How well he knew that the promise was conditional on the action being in the will of God. How he longed for the body of Jesus to be smashed, spread-eagled on the ground below.

Step outside the will of God and disaster must be the result. Satan's arguments can be so clever for he is a better theologian than any of us – but he remains the Devil.

Jesus used two weapons to secure his victory. He stood firm on Scripture and operated in the power of the Holy Spirit. He repeated, 'It is written', trusting the Word of God which proceeds from the Holy Spirit (Acts 1:16; 28:25).

As we spend time reading God's word, the Holy Spirit leads us not only to understand the truth but also to live the truth. The Holy Spirit cannot tolerate sin. So his power is available to keep us separate from Satan's superficial offers. It is this 'Spirit of holiness' (Rom 1:4, NIV) who is the one God has placed within us in order that we may stand and grow in him.

'God keeps his promise, and he will not allow you to be tested beyond your power to remain firm; at the time you are put to the test, he will give you the strength to endure it and so provide you with a way out' (1 Cor 10:13).

What is the Holy Spirit seeking to achieve? This will not always be obvious but he often allows the Devil to overreach himself by taking hold of our struggles and employing them to fulfil his own supreme purpose. The unavoidable conclusion is that God allows us to be tempted in order that he may begin to see our lives more perfectly reflecting the love and character of his Son. In other words, his ultimate intention is that each one of us might daily more clearly resemble Jesus.

Where the Holy Spirit observes areas of weakness in our lives, he acts in the same manner as a Peruvian potter. The potter flicks the rim of a pot and listens for the ring that proclaims a perfect glaze. If the sound is wrong, he places the pot back in the oven until the fire has done its work. Only when the tone is perfect will it be passed as a fit vessel for regular usage. In our lives, God will highlight our areas of weakness. This is the same way that, in the wilderness, Israel came under the spotlight of God's own search for right living among his people. Instead of yielding to God's authority and receiving his aid they were to fail in their response to temptation – and to do so time and time again. That was the reason that, after crossing the Red Sea, they took forty years to complete a fortnight's journey. God longed to take them into the Promised Land but the majority ended as bleached bones in the desert.

It can be exactly the same for us. Temptation is not sin. God can use it to mould our lives but our failure to respond as Jesus intends means that we may have to face going over the same ground for lap after lap until we finally surrender to his love and authority in our lives. For the Holy Spirit will not be content until all those hardened areas of failure within us, those long-continued weaknesses, have been changed by his love and power.

'When the devil had finished all this tempting, he left him until an opportune time' (Luke 4:13, NIV). Having led him into the wilderness, the Holy Spirit had initiated a vital process in the life of Jesus. An ongoing narrative of victory over Satan had been established and the anointing of the Spirit at his baptism was now proved to be real. Jesus entered the wilderness 'full of the Spirit'. Triumphing over Satan, he 'returned to Galilee in the power of the Spirit' (Luke 4:14). It was fulness that led to power. The result was a defeated Satan and the years of triumph had begun.

Because Jesus had been completely victorious on a cross and because we, too, know that same Holy Spirit, there is an inescapable conclusion. By living in obedience to the will of Jesus for our lives, and through the power of his Spirit within us, we also will enjoy victory over the powers and the deceptions of the Devil.

Chapter 8

Danger – Powers at play

All around the world there are particular countries that, in recent years, have managed either to attract or repel their wealthier neighbours – and with significant results.

Haiti is a good case in point. Only thirty years ago, when compared to the neighbouring Dominican Republic, Haiti's future looked bright. Today that has changed. Her once burgeoning tourist industry has collapsed in ruins and whole sections of her economy appear to be shattered. Occasionally attempts are made to change things, but scepticism is the normal response for any claims that Haiti is now a budding and emergent democracy. The main reason is that corruption still seems to rule as confidently as ever. As far as violence goes, it is certainly not safe to walk the streets alone by night and it can even be dangerous in the daytime. At fifteen years of age, my youngest daughter Suzy was being driven along the streets of Port-au-Prince and the vehicle passed a man who had just been murdered. It was only around midday!

If you take a plane flight across the island, then the boundary line between Haiti and the Dominican Republic is obvious. As you look down, it is plain to see, for the trees on the Haiti side of the border have been indiscriminately felled and only scrubland remains. It all stands in stark contrast to the Dominican Republic's greater political stability, relatively thriving tourist industry, developing economy and lush trees and foliage!

As I walked out of filming a section of one of Haiti's quasi-voodoo ceremonies, specially designed for the more adventurous type of tourist with a hunger for the bizarre side of life, I felt repelled by what I had just witnessed. The feelings of disgust did not come because I was a mature Westerner who knew that this was all a fake. Instead I was nauseated because these things were a shadow of those powers that have dominated Haiti for so long.

The camera crew joined me as we made our way down towards one of Haiti's largest churches. I stood outside and simply explained to the camera that I am an Englishman, and therefore I come from a country that has had experience of witchcraft in its history. I certainly have no difficulty believing in the existence of the Devil. However, like a former voodoo priest whom we also interviewed, I may be convinced about Satan's existence but I am even firmer in my conviction about Satan's downfall.

To my mind, there is absolutely no doubt that when darkness suddenly descended upon a crude Roman cross outside a Jerusalem rubbish dump some two thousand years ago, the death of Jesus changed the course of world history.

The amazing truth is that as Satan gazed upon the earth, he saw one solitary individual who lived a life that was totally filled in every part by the Holy Spirit. Looking frankly and objectively at what then happened, the impartial observer is almost forced to the conclusion that the Devil panicked. As he breathed a sigh of relief at the sight of the Son of God hanging upon a cross, he could scarcely have realised that within a few short weeks, that one man would have commissioned the beginnings of a mighty army.

Now the power and finality of death had been clearly conquered. Those moments when darkness fell witnessed the Son of God on a cross as he chose to surrender his life. The result was that his sacrifice of himself was to usher in the dawning of a whole new era in human experience for within three short days, the grave was empty and a dead man was making a surprise appearance to his astounded followers. Only six weeks later, in an upper room, the Holy Spirit arrived in tongues of flame. His dramatic entrance initiated a world-changing strategy, because he would bring to the disciples of Jesus the power to change their world. From this moment on, he would come to live with all those ordinary men and women who surrendered themselves to Jesus Christ and would remain with them as an indwelling power transforming their lives, both now and for eternity.

None of this could ever have been possible apart from the cross. Only there could divine forgiveness meet the requirements of divine holiness. On a cross, heaven's love and justice met – and embraced. Now the Spirit would come to forgiven lives. Now God's purposes would be fulfilled among the Gentiles. Now the Church would emerge as a covenant people of God. Now the good news of saving faith in Jesus would spread throughout the earth. Motivated by his love for humankind, and supremely by his desire to do his Father's will, Jesus paid on the nail the price of our sins. He died on a cross out of love for us. This single event clearly and finally initiated Satan's downfall.

As I tried to explain this truth, it finally dawned on me that the real problem for Haiti did not ultimately lie in its form of government, its economy, its corruption, its incipient violence or anything else. As other countries rejected Haitian pleas for help for these reasons, they were actually missing the point. These were only symptoms rather than the real cause. For the spiritual darkness that pervades Haiti pervades every area of its national life. That is why the Haitian churches have begun to take action against the voodoo past that has permeated its society.

The problem for Christians who do not want to remain silent about their faith lies in knowing how to begin to attempt to convince a world that is so totally obsessed by materialism and physical realities that there really is another dimension to life. Related to this is the fact that in seeing the material as an independent reality, we fail to recognise that spiritual powers can often be the invisible pianist playing upon a clearly visible piano.

Many people have known that slightly eerie moment when they sensed that they had encountered something 'out there.'

Within the Western world, we find ourselves living in a society which desperately wants to believe that something can only exist if it can be heard, touched, tasted, seen or smelt. That is quite simply what the vast majority of those who live around us feels that it ought to believe. A basic part of the reason for this is that we live in the aftermath of a nineteenth and twentieth century materialistic worldview which laid enormous stress on the encouragement of scientific and technological development.

This view had developed from the optimistic assumption that modern man was very different from his predecessors and would therefore very shortly 'come of age' and would institute a glorious 'brave new world'. Great stress was therefore placed upon the importance of our exercising tolerance, reasonableness and strictly human common sense in order that as humankind we might be able to fulfil our great potential.

The idea was that 'God', if indeed one had ever existed, had created this world as an elaborate mechanical device which he had wound up once like a giant clockwork toy, and had then excused himself to go off to other activities, leaving this world to fend for itself. Our small world was therefore now little more than a totally independent closed entity locked off from a God who was no longer concerned with the affairs of humankind.

It became only too easy to conclude that 'Materialism Rules, OK?'

If God were gone?

If God had effectively locked himself out of this world, then the possibility of supernatural intervention in the affairs of this world had departed with him. He was to be replaced by self-reliance. In his absence, the inevitable conclusion was that we must ourselves represent the only real hope for the future. Only the present material world was viewed as having reality. There could be no divine, miraculous or supernatural forces in the universe. Many recognised that forces existed which defied human explanation; they simply denied that these could be supernatural in origin. If an unseen, non-material world were to exist, then it could be little more than a figment of Steven Spielberg's imagination.

Such views prevailed throughout the first half of the twentieth century then popular support for this perspective began to wane. The problem was that after two World Wars, the origination of the atomic bomb, starvation on a worldwide scale and a raging AIDS epidemic of global proportions, the Utopian dream had begun to look like a hollow sham.

This has now been replaced by a growing and genuine hunger for spiritual realities and fulfilment. This can be seen in the incredible growth of astrology, Eastern religions, new cults, occultism and transcendental meditation. Just a few years ago, the majority of observers would probably have dismissed all of these as crude, simplistic and infantile. Now this odd 'smorgasbord' of quasi-religious experimental practices is dignified by the name 'New Age' and has become the fresh faith for millions of people. So 'reason' is now out and 'experience' back in, the only difference being that now the experience no longer even has to be reasonable.

There were other grounds for this replacement's appearing to be quite unsatisfactory. A fascination with occultism, and even with its potential entertainment value, has begun both to occupy and to consume the minds of many people. Nowhere is this more evident than among children. Some estimates of experimentation with the occult in Britain conclude that over seventy per cent of fifteen-year-olds have experimented for themselves with ouija boards, levitation or séances.

The concept of 'power' was understood by both ancient and more primitive modern cultures as representing the 'coming together of spiritual and material factors'. Over the last few hundred years, within the Western world, the notion of 'power' has been related to 'material power'. It has become completely unfashionable to consider that spirits, gods, ghosts or demons could in any way be regarded as the agents behind powerful happenings in our world. We now confidently assume that when ancient civilisations talked of gods, spirits or powers, their ideas were rooted in ignorance, psychological factors, mass hallucination or simply lack of proper medical knowledge. Our preference today is for a more rational approach based upon the physical laws of the universe that have now been revealed by modern science.

The concept of a personal God is seen as being neither real nor relevant. All modern society requires is to ensure a consistent advance in scientific understanding in order that human reason can devise its own answers to the problems confronting us.

One side-result of this is that any sense of need for a personal God has been reduced to a level that is neither real nor relevant, let alone desirable. It has become generally accepted that a consistent advance in scientific understanding can meet all the needs of modern society. After all, human reason can quite adequately produce its own answers to the whole gamut of problems which may confront humankind. The result has been that more and more people are no longer looking to external sources for their support. Modern man has become a quintessentially self-reliant being.

The gods of our age?

Materialism has therefore tended to fix a rigid boundary between the Creator and his creation. Technological growth has provided the confirmation for most people that God is no longer necessary for life in a modern world. After all, who needs a healer, even a miracle-worker, when there is a hospital just down the road?

While many believe that there are no divine or supernatural forces in existence in the universe, they are forced to concede that there are many things that, quite frankly, we do not understand. There is too much around which simply defies the human imagination. It has been quite easy to affirm that when a car breaks down, this is more likely to be due to a mechanical fault than mischievous djinn needing to be cast out of the machinery. However, the results of a private séance or the exercise of astral projection often lie outside the realm of rational explanation. The same applies to overseas phenomena such as the practice of voodoo in Haiti and activities associated with the spirit world in African tribal religions. A person may consider the concept of 'the powers' the product of simple people's imagination. He may relegate the concept to the level of a myth but then become so fascinated by the existence of the unknown that these 'powers' are given a status which would be denied if people simply stopped to think about what they were doing. France for example, as the epitome of a modern materialistic society, today has more psychic mediums per head of population than any other Western nation.

Our lives are full of unanswered questions. These tend to include problem areas such as:

What follows death?

Why does each tribe and culture select something or someone to worship?

From where does our human creativity emerge?

When will I understand the human inner personal desire to uncover the transcendent, to find something 'out there'?

Such questions all defy our desire for easy answers. As a result the French philosopher Blaise Pascal concluded that 'reason's last step is the recognition that there is an infinite number of things which are beyond it. It is merely feeble if it does not go as far as to realise that.' The redundancy of our human capacity to explain our world has, at long last, arrived.

The problem with being faced with so many unanswered questions and with having so many unexplained mysteries is that the gaps in our understanding have left plenty of room for fantasy and superstition to complement what was already a thoroughly corrupt picture. Steven Spielberg found a winning formula when he directed films in which action-packed scenes were placed in a fantasy framework. He made his fortune from the Indiana Jones trilogy where supernatural powers constantly intruded into 'Boys' Own'-style adventure stories. No rational explanation was offered as to the power of the Holy Grail, an idol temple or the awesome concentration of spiritual energy that was contained in his fictitious Ark of the Covenant. Their very impossibility produced a sense of fascination. Yet the way in which these were so closely related to real situations was cleverly designed to heighten the sense of intrigue by taking them out of the realm of science fiction and into the twilight zone of what could be if certain 'powers' were real. At the same time, each was designed to simply defy natural reason and to keep viewers firmly convinced that they safely belonged only in the province of a vivid imagination.

As one twentieth-century author has concluded, 'Angels, spirits, principalities, powers, gods, Satan – these, along with all other spiritual realities, are unmentionables of our culture.

The dominant materialistic world-view has absolutely no place for them. These archaic relics of a superstitious past are unspeakable because modern secularism has massive resistance even to thinking about these phenomena, having fought so long and hard to rid itself of every vestige of transcendence.' (Walter Wink, *Unmasking the Powers*, Fortress Press, 1986).

Forces we try to ignore

Today there are still around 140 million people who follow various forms of primal religion. These commonly present society as being populated by invisible powers. They are viewed as permeating the whole of human life and existence. These unseen powers are frequently viewed as attaching themselves to ancestors, to mythological heroes, to inanimate objects such as trees and flowers or even to the wider forces of nature. A concern for personal welfare and for the well-being of the community means that such 'forces' must be kept happy, and because they are regarded as conferring personal safety, success and failure, must be constantly appeased.

The use of magic and ritual, usually facilitated by specialists such as pagan priests or witchdoctors, is often viewed as an essential part of life. Only by such means can protection be acquired against the mischievous activities of malevolent spirits. It is easy to joke about such beliefs but their influence remains strong in many societies – and with strongly negative results.

I never anticipated the reception that I received in one village in Mozambique. Frankly, I was a little embarrassed to receive a hero's welcome upon entering a village that I had never visited before. It was only when the tribal elders explained that it was my staff who had earned this honour for me that I began to understand, and in response to my questions, the story slowly unfolded.

Linda Ngzane was an African nurse on our staff. She had begun to operate a 'child survival' programme for us in that part of the country. When she visited this particular village, she discovered the high percentage of children under five years of age who were dying from diarrhoea. The people simply accepted this as a fact of life. It was a problem that had been with them for decades. Whenever a child fell sick they followed the instructions given to them by the witchdoctors. A bowl of water would be placed outside the family's hut and a damp cloth would be used to wipe the child's bottom. Afterwards the cloth was placed in the bowl of water. After each bout of diarrhoea the process would be repeated. Every night a portion of the water from the bowl was carefully measured out, diluted a little, then given to the child to drink. The bowl of water was retained overnight and the next morning this routine would continue. Eventually the baby or young child would be reduced to being forced to drink barely diluted diarrhoea. The inevitable result was that many died.

Linda became quite desperate because this practice had traditionally received the backing of the tribal elders. Few would have dared to defy the witchdoctor's instructions. Patiently Linda worked to convince the mothers that this was all wrong. Eventually she succeeded. The bowl of diarrhoea became replaced by a simple salt solution and the children began to survive. The question remains as to who on earth would have originated such a vile and evil way of doing things? Was it pure ignorance or did more malevolent forces play their own part in creating this tragedy?

So where are the Powers?

The Bible clearly disagrees with the conclusions of human reason. Rather than falling into the trap of adopting the 'either...or' mentality of materialism and primal religions the Bible chooses to adopt a 'both...and' understanding. It chooses to speak of the powers in a variety of ways. They are both:

Heavenly and earthly

Human and divine

Spiritual and political

Invisible and structural

This is why the whole concept of the powers is so difficult to understand, and because we cannot devise a neat little box in which to place them we can be guilty of ignoring them. For the Bible does not present us with tidy distinctions in relation to unseen spirits. Scripture does not lead us to conclude that demons are the direct cause of all sicknesses, now only to be treated by physicians and psychiatrists. Nor does it suggest that principalities and powers are merely socio-political structures, now to be the sole concern of politicians, economists and sociologists. Instead Scripture sees the physical and spiritual as being often intermingled, and presents us with many vivid pictures of forces at work in our world - forces that are clearly beyond our human control.

That is the reason why sickness may be (and usually is) a purely physical ailment, but we cannot put it past the 'enemy of our souls' to employ physical means to attack us. In the same way 'powers' will usually refer to actual human agencies such as social systems, secular authorities and political structures. Yet it can be the case that these physical institutions will have spiritual forces acting as a controlling influence upon them (see Matt 20:25; Mark 10:42; Luke 22:25; Acts 4:26).

These forces are not merely powerful. The ways in which they are described often amount to little less than a definition of power itself. Words the Bible employs about them include names such as 'principalities', 'powers' and 'thrones'. These clearly refer to superhuman powers (Rom 8:38; Eph 6:12; Col 1:16; 2:15), and yet the same words are used elsewhere to describe human rulers (Luke 12:11; Acts 4:26). On other occasions, the distinction in Scripture is even less clear and these words could describe either human or supernatural forces (Rom13:1; 1 Cor 2:8; Titus 3:1).

So the Bible recognises the reality of both human authority and spiritual powers. It also depicts situations where spiritual powers greatly influence human authority and the two operate together, although often without the human agency even being aware of the fact. It often seems that Christians are only too ready and willing to accept the involvement of evil forces when their activity can actually be observed – as, for instance, when someone displays obvious signs of suffering from demonic manifestations. However, where the alternative exists of a straightforward human explanation, this often appears far preferable to the suggestion of sinister spiritual influences being at work.

To many people it seems naïve and fanciful to suggest that issues such as apartheid and slavery could have their origins in the work of some unseen power. Both of these practices sought to achieve the degradation, humiliation, oppression, suffering and practical enslavement of millions of people. Both had their roots in economic greed, false pride, fear, self-interest and a distorted interpretation of Scripture. It is true that human beings carried out these dreadful practices but it is equally difficult to ignore the possibility that they were motivated by forces beyond themselves. Once we have come to acknowledge that powerful spiritual realities exist beyond ourselves, then to see a diabolic strategy behind these awful deeds can scarcely be regarded as blind fantasy. After all, Scripture does warn us that, 'The god of this age has blinded ... minds' (2 Cor 4:4, NIV).

Where are the powers? The Bible declares that they are all around us. It refers to angels of light (Ps 91:11; Matt 4:6; Heb 1:4-7) and to those myriad angels that chose to follow Satan in his rebellion against God and form the nucleus of his demon forces (Matt 12:22-29; Luke 8:30-38; Rev 16:13,14). These demons may attach themselves to specific territories or practices (Dan 10:13; 12:1 and following verses). They appear to be equally at home in 'the pit' (Luke 8:31), which is probably where we would most expect to find them, or in 'the air' (Eph 2:2), from which strategic vantage point they are ready and able to harass humankind. These conquered Satanic powers have yet to be tamed and domesticated. While they have no choice but to acknowledge the victory of Jesus over them, they still remain in a state of active rebellion against him (Phil 2:10). While their ultimate defeat has already been secured through the power of crucified love, they will still attempt to exercise their pervasive influence over structures and individuals alike.

Opposing the Powers

One fact of which most of us would probably wish to remain in a state of blissful ignorance is that the Holy Spirit does not normally go into battle alone. The uncomfortable fact is that the Holy Spirit usually enters into combat with enemy powers by working in and through the people of God. Now we might well wish that we were simply not involved but the truth of the matter is that we were not recruited into the armies of the living God in order to engage in civilian pursuits. However unpleasant it may seem, the fact is that sometimes we are intended to go to war.

It is significant to note that when the Apostle Paul instructs us to 'put on the full armour of God' (Eph 6:13) and therefore to prepare for battle, none of the armour which God has provided is designed to protect our backs. It all operates on the assumption that we will always be moving forwards. We are called upon to stand as the army of God marching together under divine direction to share in the Spirit's victory over the powers.

The reason for our boldness lies in the sense of security that we have found in knowing that the one sure antidote against the powers lies in the blood of Jesus Christ and the power of his Holy Spirit. It is here that true spiritual authority can be found and experienced. So while we might have wished that we could remain as spiritual pacifists – at least we can know that we are on the winning side. Jesus made a public example of the powers from a cross. He unmasked these hidden forces as enemies of the living God and demonstrated that while the Roman system of justice and the Jewish religious structures were mere puppets of powers more mighty than themselves, Jesus could reign over them from a tree.

It was from a cross that Jesus triumphed over the powers. Then in his resurrection by the Holy Spirit, he actually penetrated and captured their territory. Jesus had successfully invaded the realm of destruction and death and inflicted a resounding and total defeat upon the principalities and powers on their own home ground.

As Canon Michael Green has so acutely observed, 'In Christ they were created (Col 1:16) and in Christ they were defeated

(Col 2:15). Philippians 2:10 makes it quite plain that they must own his sway whether they like it or not. His Lordship, since the resurrection, has been beyond cavil among beings celestial, terrestrial and subterranean' (Michael Green, *I Believe in Satan's Downfall*, Hodder, 1981).

It is true that spiritual warfare does incorporate some similarities with physical conflicts. However, we need to be careful not to take the analogy too far, for while one depends largely on physical strength and the necessary equipment for doing battle, the weapons of the other war are those of compassion and self-giving love.

One good illustration of where we need to put these principles to work in doing battle with the powers lies in the field of economics. The powers will always attempt to foster an unfair distribution of resources so that the 'haves' seize more and the 'have nots' receive less. By this means, they can create further injustice and cultivate resentment and bitterness. Their goals are always quite simple. Their desire is to create chaos and wreak havoc between people and nations by nurturing greed and the hunger for power. For as long as Western societies regard the availability of goods to purchase, economic prosperity and the power that comes with it as constituting the ultimate goals for a nation, the powers will already have won one half of the battle.

But this is not just a problem that faces nations; it concerns us equally as individuals. Too great a commitment to the accumulation of financial wealth, and a wrong estimate of its importance, is sternly denounced in the Bible. Jesus warned his disciples, 'Guard yourselves from every kind of greed; because a person's true life is not made up of the things he owns, no matter how rich he may be' (Luke 12:15). A society that equates a good standard of living with the money an individual has available at the time is sadly out of kilter with what Jesus had to say on the matter. He pointed out the inconsistency in the idea that Christianity and materialism can ever be comfortable bedfellows when he observed that, 'No one can be a slave of two masters ... You cannot serve both God and money' (Matt 6:24).

In Old Testament times God declared war on poverty. He

announced that he was against a society where poverty was tolerated. It was a command rather than a prophecy when he instructed Israel, 'Not one of your people will be poor' (Deut 15:4). Jesus himself lived in a state of relative poverty and he had some pretty tough things to say to the rich. It is always important to remember that it was when Zacchaeus offered generous compensation to those from whom he had embezzled and extorted money that Jesus could exclaim, 'Salvation has come to this house today' (Luke 19:9).

While the Holy Spirit has certainly not been given necessarily to make us poor, he has come to sensitise us to the poverty of others and the need to be actively involved in supporting and caring for all those who have more material needs than ourselves. As part of my work in the United States, I have had to point out so often that it is not ultimately a matter of what we have as a gift from God, but that what is much more important is the attitude we maintain towards our possessions and the generosity of spirit with which we are prepared to give them away.

While we are called to challenge and expose those injustices that are generated by the powers, we do also have another calling of God on our lives. For while there certainly are things that we can do, above all there are areas that can be dealt with only by God himself and therefore we are called upon to pray strongly, vigorously, and continuously. Because the powers are evil we must look and pray to the one who is good in order that their strategies might be thwarted.

We are called upon not only to confront injustice but also to pray. If we are to engage in effective spiritual warfare in this way, we will not achieve it on our own. We will need the Holy Spirit's enabling if we are to pray effectively. Scripture does place all of our spiritual abilities and resources in the simple context of our learning how to 'pray in the Spirit on all occasions' (Eph 6:18, NIV).

Often I think that our failure to recognise the existence of supernatural forces is equalled only by our failure to recognise the power that is available to us in prayer. It is fair to ask whether major world events such as wars, man-made disasters, famine, civil unrest and many others might have happened differently, or even have been avoided, if only the Church had risen up to face her God-given challenge of interceding on behalf of others? If we had learned what it means to accept the responsibility of praying constantly in the Holy Spirit, then what would the God of heaven have accomplished on the earth? One has to really wonder what God would do in response to his Church praying in this way.

This may seem somewhat far removed from our normal and rather casual sense of spiritual experience. It just may not fit in with the values or even the priorities that we currently adopt in our local church or fellowship. We may have been under the mistaken impression that the Holy Spirit was simply there to make our spiritual lives more fun and more fulfilling. Yet we often gaze in despair at the society that surrounds us and bemoan the condition into which it has fallen. We miss out on the point that this is the end-result of enemy activity and that we have been called to do something about it.

It is only in our prayer, whether it be alone or with others, that we can encounter these realities. It is only as we pray that we can unlock the gates of heaven and see the living God release his grace and power upon us again. Human energies are completely inadequate for warfare against the powers. We have to realise that we can only see the triumph of Jesus re-enacted among us as we pray in the power of the Holy Spirit.

It is not sufficient for us to be content with murmuring a routine or ritual prayer on behalf of those in government. Paul insisted that spiritual warfare should be a reality in our experience, and Jesus pointed out that a successful invasion of opposition territory is dependent upon our first being able to bind and immobilise the strong man (Matt 12:24–29; Eph 6:12). That is exactly what happens when we start to pray strong prayers. It would be naïve to think that we could ever see the rooting out of injustice and victory over the powers by any other means.

A successful combating of the attempted interference from evil powers will only take place when we engage in the regular activity of committed intercession in the way that God intended. Whenever injustice is faced in the world as the result of the powers being at work, then the measure of our concern for the poor and the powerless can be seen not just in the level of our giving or through our personal involvement but in how we pray. For whenever Satan uses his minions to seek to frustrate the work of God, then prayer is the immediate and appropriate defence in the face of enemy attack. When the powers strike, then we are called to strike back. Being involved in the American version of Tearfund is an exciting challenge. Pretty well everything is done differently from the way we did things in Britain. It is great to be able to witness the lives of so many people around the world being transformed, both physically and spiritually, through the care and support of the churches. Yet the enemy does always try to interfere and naturally enough, one of his prime targets will always be those occasions when decisions are being taken over the future direction of the work. So whenever our Board meets, we can legitimately anticipate that spiritual warfare may be taking place.

Recently we appointed a delightful African-American couple to act as the full-time prayer coordinators for World Relief. Although they both possessed quite a chequered history, this couple knew the Lord intimately and just loved to pray. They appreciated only too well the nature and reality of spiritual warfare. For that reason, they anticipated that the enemy would want to get involved and interfere with our Board's decisions. So for the duration of the Board meetings they parked themselves in the corridor outside the room in which the Board was conducting its deliberations, and started to pray. Except for meal and loo breaks, they stayed there for the entire thirty-six hours that the Board was together.

Imagine the surprise of many Board members when walking along the corridor they saw this couple, with any staff members they could find, praying their hearts out for the Board. One is forced to ask whether it is mere coincidence that our Board meetings are becoming more and more effective and encouraging. And the next area of enquiry would probably include asking who it is that plays the major role – the Chairman, the Executive Director or the prayer warriors?

Before Jesus confronted the powers in the most strategic moments of his ministry here on earth, he paused to pray. We are not called to run away from spiritual conflict or to ignore the plight of those for whom the very survival of themselves and their families is at risk on a daily basis. Instead we are called upon to follow in the footsteps of that one who demonstrated that the very opposite of Satanic power can be seen in a baby laid in a manger and a man dying unjustly on a cross. His life supremely showed that compassion towards others and the sense of prayerful dependence on his Father which caused the powers to shudder.

Whatever the powers may seek to throw at us, it is his example that we must follow. It is in order that we may live our lives for him that we are equipped by the Holy Spirit. It is in his service that we take our stand.

Chapter 9

Gifted by God

When my children were young, I would often come home from a trip and bring them presents. Although this was not an attempt to buy their love, it was successful in getting them to notice that I was back. However, sometimes they seemed to be more interested in the present I had brought than in the fact that I had returned. I did not object too strongly because pretty soon they would realise that a gift meant that the giver was not far away and they would turn their attention to the recognition that Daddy was home, at last! If they had ignored the gifts I'd brought them and just left them unopened, I think I might have been offended! They probably feel similarly nowadays because they have a better understanding of exactly how long it must have taken me to select, let alone discover, the right gifts for them.

The Holy Spirit is a gift from God. Yet he in turn has many gifts to give us. If any of us were to be guilty of rejecting or ignoring these gifts, then we would run the risk not only of insulting the Holy Spirit but also perhaps being the unwitting cause of damage both to ourselves and to others. For most of these gifts are not just designed to benefit us but are also intended to act as the tools for us to help other people. It is also true that when we are using the gifts which the Holy Spirit has given to us, we show most clearly the reality of what it means to be part of the Church of Jesus Christ. As Paul wrote to the Corinthian church, 'All of you are Christ's body, and each one is a part of it' (1 Cor 12:27).

Just as each part of our body has a role to play, so each one of us has a task in the body of Christ, his church. Just as a missing part in the body is instantly obvious and hampers every other part by its absence, so it is with the church.

Jesus always chose ordinary people through whom his Spirit could specifically express his gifts and love. The early church continued in the same vein. Acts 8:1 provides us with just one example among many where the phrase 'the church' is used. The only qualification to this principle is geographical, when reference is made to the church at Colossae or Corinth or Ephesus. No other distinction or division is made.

The reason? Because the body is the body of Jesus, it is not open to sub-division. This body cannot be divided into gifted and non-gifted sections. We all have a specific role to play within the purposes of God, and all of us who belong to Jesus automatically become a part of his eternal body, the Church. Yet to live up to all that God has for us will not involve travelling along a trouble-free road. He is with us and he is for us, but that does not mean that our journey will be miraculously free of difficulty. For that is so often the way that he chooses to prepare us for the rest of our lives with him.

Specifically Jesus pioneered the way for us when he taught his disciples to face up to and win over four major problems which confronted them in their daily lives.

The problem of unknown potential – Luke 10:1–24. By sending out seventy-two disciples Jesus clearly demonstrated that learning to serve him is not confined to listening to his words. By going out together, they destroyed the myth that the Lord will only use a spiritual élite. They returned full of joy because of the way the Holy Spirit had used them. But Jesus did not send them on this journey of discovery alone. They travelled in twos, developing the potential in one another – and so should we. We must always heed the warning never to attempt to live as a lone wolf for Jesus but to surrender to the divine influence of the Holy Spirit and permit him to use our friends to develop the resources which they may help to identify within our lives.

The problem of wrong comparisons – Luke 21:1–4. Many of us wonder if we are totally useless. As we look at others whom God uses, we see our gifts as totally insignificant. But Jesus showed that the poor widow who offered a couple of coins gave a more meaningful offering than any of the leaders contributing large sums of money which they could easily afford.

The problem of over-competitiveness – Luke 9:46–48. Jesus overturned all arguments as to who was the greatest among his disciples. We cannot compete for gifts because it is the Holy Spirit who makes them available to us. If we are to stop devaluing ourselves and trust God's Spirit for all that we need for service, then we must similarly be careful to check that we take no undue credit for his activities in our lives. What God chooses to do in the lives of his unlikely servants should bring credit to the Lord, not to us ourselves.

The problem of fear – Luke 10:30-37. In the story of the Good Samaritan, we see how easy it is to decline God's gifts and opportunities for service because we are afraid of the consequences. Somehow we prefer a quiet life to a useful one. When the King of Kings was hung up on a cross, he did not allow this to happen to him in order that he might gain a bunch of insipid and frightened disciples – they were that already. Instead, the purpose of Jesus was always to die and to save those who would, by the power of his Holy Spirit, possess lives so revolutionised that, as his people, they would speak his word with boldness and witness the transformation of their own society as their world was being turned upside down.

Who are these gifts for?

The simple answer is – us!

An old story describes a Christian arriving at the gates of heaven. He was warmly greeted by the Archangel Gabriel who offered a personally guided tour around the vastness of heaven. The first building they visited was an enormous aircraft hangar lined with narrow shelves. Each shelf was filled with neatly wrapped presents, all addressed to the new arrival.

'What's this, then?' inquired the Christian.

'Oh, those,' replied Gabriel, 'they're all the gifts which God had for you to use on earth and which you never bothered to claim!'

This perhaps explains why the teaching of Scripture is so plain and forceful on this point. The Apostle Paul writes to the church at Rome, 'Do not think of yourself more highly than you should ... We have many parts in the one body and all these parts have different functions. In the same way, though we are many, we are one body in union with Christ and we are all joined to each other as different parts of one body. So we are to use our different gifts in accordance with the grace that God has given us. If our gift is to speak God's message, we should do it according to the faith that we have; if it is to serve, we should serve; if it is to teach, we should teach; if it is to encourage others, we should do so. Whoever shares with others should do it generously; whoever has authority should work hard; whoever shows kindness to others should do it cheerfully' (Rom 12:3–8).

There can surely be no more tragic obituary than 'He ignored God's gifts and so failed to serve as he could have done.'

What are these gifts?

Several gifts are mentioned in the New Testament, although Christians are not agreed on the exact number. Consequently the following list of those mentioned in the New Testament is not meant to be exhaustive. Some have argued that God is raising up other gifts especially applicable to life in our world today. Still this list should provide us with a pretty good starting point. There are those who would suggest that these gifts lost their value or even died out completely after the Scriptures were completed. But if this were true, then it is at least strange that the Scriptures themselves make no mention of the possibility. Anyway, these twenty-seven gifts clearly played a basic part in the life, ministry and spiritual equipment of the local church during the first century of its existence.

1. The gift of discerning of spirits (1 Cor 12:10. See Luke 8:29).
2. The gift of the word of knowledge (1 Cor 12:8. See Luke 18:22).
3. The gift of the word of wisdom (1 Cor 12:8. See Luke 6:9).
4. The gift of tongues (Acts 19:6; 1 Cor 12:10; 14:13–33).
5. The gift of prophecy (1 Thess 5:20,21).
6. The gift of interpretation of tongues (1 Cor 14:13).
7. The gift of healing (1 Cor 12:9. See Acts 28:1–10).
8. The gift of faith (1 Cor 12:9. See Acts 3:6).

9. The gift of miracles (1 Cor 12:10. See Acts 6:8).
10. The gift of service (Rom 12:7. See 2 Tim 1:16–18).
11. The gift of teaching (Eph 4:13,14).
12. The gift of motivation (Rom 12:8. See Acts 20:18–31).
13. The gift of giving (Rom 12:8. See Acts 4:32–35).
14. The gift of leadership (Rom 12:8. See Acts 13:1–2).
15. The gift of mercy (Rom 12:8. See Luke 5:12,13).
16. The gift of apostle (Eph 4:11).
17. The gift of hospitality (1 Pet 4:9).
18. The gift of celibacy (1 Cor 7:8).
19. The gift of administration (Acts 6:2,3).
20. The gift of exorcism (Acts 16:18).
21. The gift of evangelism (Eph 4:11; 2 Tim 4:5).
22. The gift of pastoral guidance (Eph 4:11).
23. The gift of being a missionary (Eph 3:7).
24. The gift of being willing to face martyrdom (1 Cor 13:3).
25. The gift of helping (1 Cor 12:28).
26. The gift of intercession (Rom 8:26,27).
27. The gift of encouragement (Rom 12:8. See Heb 10:24,25).

Each one of us is individual and different in God's sight so he equips us with different gifts. Each gift is unique in itself although many can be employed alongside each other in complementary fashion. Gifts can normally be repeated although martyrdom is clearly a one-off! There is such a variety to choose from and most of us are not limited to the possession of just one single gift. In fact, I could suggest that if you can only identify one of these gifts in your life, then you may have it in abundance!

What are they for?

'The Church is Christ's body' (Eph 1:23) so it is a living organism in which Christ is the head and each one of us should be a vitally functioning part.

The gifts of the Holy Spirit are given by God to enable the members of the Body of Christ to function properly.

The gifts of the Holy Spirit are given by God to enable the active participation of all the members of the body of Christ.

The gifts of the Holy Spirit represent the bounty of God and are designed to demonstrate, within the Body of Christ, the beauty of God.

As Simon Magus discovered in his confrontation with Simon Peter, a gift is a gift. We cannot buy it or earn it nor should we use it for our own selfish purposes. It is to be used as God directs. Peter was both quick and direct in his response, 'May you and your money go to hell, for thinking that you can buy God's gift with money! You have no part or share in our work because your heart is not right in God's sight' (Acts 8:20,21).

What do we know about them?

Gifts are there to be received but they are also intended to be used. God has entrusted them to us in order that they might be employed for the building of his Kingdom, not merely for our own fulfilment or entertainment. For us the privilege of our having them involves the responsibility of our using them properly.

Because each and every Christian has, and must be account-able for one or more gifts, our commitment to God is seen as becoming concrete and tangible in the manner in which we handle those gifts which have been entrusted to us. As Elizabeth O'Connor has commented, 'Commitment at the point of my gifts means that I must give up being a straggler.' Our responsibility therefore extends to discovering, developing and using our gifts. Inspired by the Holy Spirit, the Apostle Peter clearly instructs his readers that 'each one, as a good manager of God's different gifts, must use for the good of others the special gift he has received from God' (1 Pet 4:10).

Gifts are part of a 'three-way giving'. God gives them to us, we offer them back to God, and by his Spirit he equips us to make them available to the whole church. This is because the church is a body and therefore a living organism. Christ is the head and, through his Spirit, makes each one of us vitally functioning parts!

Gifts are not the same as natural abilities. Everybody possesses these but when a life is committed to Jesus Christ natural talents can often become gifts because they are 'saved' along with the rest of a personality. A gift is an ability given to an individual by God out of his love and kindness, or 'grace'. The Greek word *charismata* means 'grace gifts' and, within the strict meaning of the word, denotes every Christian as a 'charismatic'. A ministry is the prolonged exercise of a gift. A gift is received rather than achieved, and ministry means serving; a ministry is therefore serving the body with the gift which God has given.

Gifts are permanent because God never takes back what he has given. 'For God does not change his mind about whom he chooses and blesses' (Rom 11:29). Our responsibility lies in the discovery, development and usage of God's gifts. So Paul encourages the Roman Christians 'to use our different gifts in accordance with the grace that God has given us' (Rom 12:6). This is because it is God's will and our welfare which are at stake!

Gifts will often overlap. An itinerant preacher could exhibit the gifts of missionary, evangelist, teacher and prophet on the same weekend in a local church. Many will combine gifts such as motivation and administration in the same personality. In a special course at the Fuller School of World Mission, Carl Cronje taught as follows:

'Gifts must be distinguished from baseline responsibilities that all of us share equally, e.g. all must pray, all must give, all must believe but over and above the prayer that is demanded of all there is the gift of intercession; over and above the giving and believing required of all there is a gift of giving and a gift of faith. Gifts then are built on the baseline, they are the areas where we do far more than the minimum requirement. They are the areas where we find ourselves very comfortable in the Lord. They are the things that make us tick, the itch that only subsides when we scratch it with involvement and commitment. We are "in our element" when we are in our gifts!'

Gifts are not to be graded. No one gift is more spiritual than another. As Paul concludes, 'So then, the eye cannot say to the hand, "I don't need you!" ... On the contrary, we cannot do without the part of the body that seems to be weaker.' Paul's whole point in 1 Corinthians 12 is that we should not regard the more seemingly 'supernatural' gifts like speaking in tongues as superior to gifts which may seem more ordinary, like helping others and administration (1 Cor 12:28). Nor should we be overconcerned about receiving false gifts. It is true that Satan can and does counterfeit God's gifts. But if our lives are totally surrendered to Jesus then he is the one from whom we receive.

Jesus told his disciples, 'As bad as you are, you know how to give good things to your children. How much more, then, will the Father in heaven give the Holy Spirit to those who ask him!' (Luke 11:13).

What must we do to use them?

A friend of mine sometimes sings a song entitled 'God likes me'. These words always provoke a reaction. It seems impossible that, with all our failures and weaknesses, God should actually care about us, let alone entrust us with his gifts! Yet he has done so and in the story of those servants to whom their master gave talents for their use, Jesus provides a warning that one day we will be accountable for how we have used them.

I don't know if you share with me a distrust of 'Teach Yourself' books and easy systems? Under normal circumstances, I would never advocate a 'how to discover your spiritual gifts' theory. Yet we desperately need to be practical on this subject and I would encourage you to examine this system and use it wherever you may find it relevant in your own life.

In his excellent book *Your Spiritual Gifts Can Make Your Church Grow*, the missiologist Peter Wagner suggests this line of discovery:

'An open mind and a teachable spirit are essentials. If we feel we know it all or are too proud to be corrected, we will not function optimally. Some practical suggestions in this regard are:

1. Explore all the possibilities by learning the Biblical facts about gifts.

2. Experiment with as many as you can. Try to find your aptitude this way. This can be done sincerely. Don't be afraid to fail. It is also important to know what gifts we don't have.

3. Examine your feelings. Your interests and your aptitudes when merging will give the greatest success. You will feel comfortable in your gift.

4. Evaluate your effectiveness. Don't be too proud to admit where you have not had success. Also don't be so (falsely) "humble" as to deny where God is using you.

5. Expect confirmation from your brothers and sisters. We are often the last to see things about ourselves that are obvious to others at a glance. This is true submission - i.e. teamwork, knowing where our boundaries of effectiveness are by mutual consultation.

6. Exert caution with regard to the particular peril of your gift. For most privileges there is a peril and this is especially true of God's gifts.'

The gifts and talents which the Holy Spirit would bring to our lives are not designed to be used in isolation. We are to complement other Christians whose gifts will be different from our own. To that end, we need to be careful to recognise those gifts that God has given to us – and those that he has not. As J B Phillips has paraphrased Romans 12:3, 'Try to have a sane estimate of your capabilities'. We should therefore be prepared to experiment and discover from the positive response (or otherwise) of other Christians whether a particular gift is really from God or the product of a fertile imagination!

I was talking to a young evangelist, who blurted out, 'I get so scared. I feel so ill before preaching, I just don't know if evangelism is my gift or not.' Now if God has really given us a gift or talent, results will inevitably follow so I asked him what response came from his preaching. 'Oh, nearly always people are converted, often several come to real repentance.' I simply encouraged him to keep feeling scared! That was a small price to pay for the privilege of using God's gift.

Another wrong concept which is current in evangelical Christianity is the idea that God only uses us in those areas where we feel uncomfortable! That is by no means usually the case. God often uses us in the areas of strength which we possess. He also can bring surprising areas of gift to us – after all he made us so he knows both who we are and what we need. It is as we place ourselves unreservedly in God's hands that he will gift us for his service. Our duty is not to do God's work for him, to ask him to bless our plans, schemes or inclinations. Instead it is to respond to God's initiatives in our lives by obedience in the gifts that he places within us.

As Peter Wagner puts it, 'Every spiritual gift we have is a resource which we must use and for which we will be held accountable at the judgement. Some will have one, some two and some five. The quantity, to begin with, does not matter. Stewards are responsible only for what the master has chosen to give them but the resource that we do have must be used to accomplish the master's purpose.'

As we open ourselves up, we cease trying to make everybody use our gifts and let them become themselves as well. We must also remember that some of our gifts will be more obvious than others and we may never cease discovering the gifts that God will add to our lives for use in the down-to-earth existence of our local fellowship and community. For it is at this level that we are supposed to demonstrate what it means truly to want to love and serve Jesus, not in our own strength but in the power and authority that God gives.

Finally, we must remember one all-important truth. Jesus, as God's greatest gift, did not come down to earth as some vague, ethereal force. The miracle of the incarnation lies in the fact that he came as a real person. It is a lesson that we must not ignore for we must never give God the use of our talents and fail to give ourselves.

Chapter 10

Gifts that sometimes cause a problem!

The Church traces its origins back to the Day of Pentecost (Acts 2:1–13). This is where it had its true start. Peter commented that the Holy Spirit came upon the Gentiles 'as he had come on us at the beginning' (Acts 11:15). Straightaway the Church recognised the Spirit as being divine. Immediately his identity and general ministry was accepted without dissension. But in many of the writings of the early Church, there is little written specifically about the Holy Spirit because he is spoken about in the context of the Trinity rather than as a specific subject in his own right.

One major exception to this general rule was the second century theologian, Ireneus. He offered his own unequivocal testimony to the importance of the Holy Spirit when he pointed out that 'Receiving the Holy Spirit, we walk in newness of life, in obedience to God. Without the Spirit of God, we cannot be saved' (quoted in Henry Bettenson, ed., *The Early Church Fathers*, Oxford University Press, 1956).

> Many of the gifts which were provided by the Holy Spirit have been joyfully accepted by God's people right down through the Christian centuries to the present day. The church has recognised these gifts in every age. But others have proved to be more controversial. Some of the gifts outlined in 1 Corinthians 12:8–10 were almost totally ignored for centuries. It has been rightly observed that, 'We ought to face the New Testament witness with sufficient candour to admit that in this ... Spirit which the Church was conscious of possessing, there lie forces of an extra-rational kind mostly lacking among us Christians today.' Somehow we ran from all that we could not understand. In so doing we reflect the spirit of the age rather than the Holy Spirit.

> We love to pattern things so that we can clearly see how, neatly packaged, they fit into our understanding. God, on the other hand, longs to see us break away from all our presuppositions, pride and prejudices. His purposes cannot be shackled to our understanding of how they should be performed!

If God is to be God, then he must reign. It is only too easy to sing words such as 'Our God Reigns' and then seek to ensure that he conforms to the way we have always operated. Our reluctance to see the Lord break through our established norms says more of our lack of flexibility and openness to his will and purpose than anything else.

Two hundred years ago, John Wesley wrote these words: 'It does not appear that these extraordinary gifts of the Holy Ghost were common in the church for more than two or three centuries. We seldom hear of them after that fatal period when the Emperor Constantine called himself a Christian ... From that time, they almost totally ceased; very few instances of the kind were found. The cause of this was not ... "because there was no more occasion for them" ... The real cause was, "the love of many", almost of all Christians, so-called, was "waxed cold"... This was the real cause why the extraordinary gifts of the Holy Ghost were no longer to be found in the Christian Church.'

These gifts can be placed in three groupings:

Gifts of Revelation (the power to know)

Discerning of spirits

Word of knowledge

Word of wisdom

Gifts for Activity (the power to do)

Gifts of healing

The working of miracles

The gift of faith

Gifts for Communication (the power to say)

The gift of tongues

The gift of interpretation

The gift of prophecy

Objection!

There are those who would stop at this point to protest. Three objections have been given to the use of these gifts today.

We don t need these gifts

The argument would be that throughout history, God worked in different ways at different times. Supernatural gifts were necessary in the early days. Now, with the completion of the Bible and the establishment of the Church, we have all we need in Scripture and have no need for further demonstration of the power of God.

There is something to be said for this line of argument, for the Spirit has been more active in some periods than in others. However, I have always felt it possesses two fatal flaws. First, it seems to be an argument based on experience rationalised by Scripture, starting with our lack of supernatural evidence and moving to our explanation. I always feel safer moving from Scripture to experience; the reverse procedure is often unreliable because instead of allowing Scripture to mould our experience, we tend to allow our defective experience to shape our interpretation. Secondly, in claiming to elevate the authority of Scripture, it fails to do justice to the truth of Scripture. There is nothing in Scripture that suggests that these gifts are not for the people of Christ in any age. An honest, penitent and expectant quest for a closer walk with God and a deeper knowledge of him will always be rooted in an understanding of all that Scripture leads us to anticipate as a part of our birthright. While conclusions will differ, we need to be careful neither to deny nor slavishly to follow the verdict of others.

These gifts focus our attention on the wrong person

The Holy Spirit does not seek to bring attention to himself, because his function is to bear witness to Jesus. The danger comes in the way that these extraordinary gifts can focus undue attention on either the Holy Spirit, the gift itself or even the person exercising the gift. Many people have been carried away with their own importance and errors have been made – but so it was in the early Church. Paul's reminders to the Corinthian Christians were designed to correct exactly that kind of mistake. But the abuse did not mean that the practice should be stopped.

One further safeguard is that these gifts should generally be practised in the context of a local church or fellowship with all the accompanying safeguards of structured authority. Scriptures give us a further standard to which our practices must conform. Finally, Christians don't follow signs; signs follow Christians.

The gifts of the Spirit are not as important as the fruit

Two Christians were talking together and one said to the other, 'Well, you can have the gifts. I'll take the fruit.' My response to that would be to suggest that I'd want to have all that God has on offer. Quite honestly, I need all the help I can get!

We need to recognise and value both fruit and gifts alike because both are produced by the Holy Spirit in the life of the believer. Each should be carefully evaluated alongside the teaching of Scripture. This is because we will never begin to understand the significance of gifts and fruit alike until we view them in the proper context of what the Bible teaches us about the Person and work of the Holy Spirit. For it is who the Holy Spirit is that determines what he does.

The simple fact is that the gifts of the Holy Spirit represent various ways in which the power of God works in and through the life of the believer. The fruit of the Holy Spirit is the character and nature of Jesus Christ being shown in the life of the believer. Therefore Jesus did not only say to the sick who came to him, 'I love you,' but he also said, 'Be healed!' Surely one of the saddest things to experience is to know what it means to love people and yet be incapable of helping them. When we are conscious of all that God is offering us, we should always be prepared to accept all that he wants to give us, even if it creates theological problems for us!

1 Corinthians 12–14 is like a sandwich, with teaching on gifts in chapters 12 and 14, and teaching on love in the middle. Sometimes people say that love is the greatest of the gifts, but this is not true to Paul's thinking which may be captured if we read 12:31 and then go on to 14:1: 'But eagerly desire the greater gifts. And now I will show you the most excellent way ... follow the way of love and eagerly desire spiritual gifts, especially the gift of prophecy.' What Paul is pleading for is the exercise of the gifts in love, the working together of the fruit and the gifts of the Spirit.

If we choose to ignore these gifts, we have to face up to the fact that we are running risks in two major areas:

By removing the supernatural ingredient from biblical Christianity, we give an open invitation to Satan to fascinate society by his own subtle but completely inferior tricks.

We can fall into the trap of reducing Christianity to the status of an alternative philosophy. The emphasis on miracles in Jesus' personal ministry encourages us to see our faith in the context of the supernatural activity of the living God among men and women.

However, as we may be unfamiliar with these gifts and because they have caused both disagreement and division due to the dangers associated with their abuse, we must look in a little more detail at what the Bible has to say about them.

Power to know

Discerning of spirits: this is different from natural judgement. It is simply the mind of Christ being revealed through a believer. This is a necessary defence, particularly where the gifts are concerned. We need to differentiate between that which comes from God, that which comes from the opposition and that which comes from our natural selves. Jesus warned his disciples not to allow themselves to be deceived: 'Be on your guard, and do not let anyone deceive you' (Matt 24:4). The warning was a necessary one. Peter could know in an instant who Jesus really was through revelation that could only have come from Father God. The next moment Jesus was having to rebuke him. 'Get away from me, Satan,' he said. 'Your thoughts don't come from God but from human nature' (Mark 8:33).

Word of knowledge: this is the supernatural revelation by God of information that was not learned by the efforts of our natural minds. We see it, for example, when Jesus sees the real need in the life of a Samaritan woman. 'Come and see the man who told me everything I have ever done' (John 4:29). This gift enabled Peter to expose corruption in the church in the case of Ananias and Sapphira (Acts 5:1–11). Often Christians experience in counselling that quiet moment when God reveals in their hearts the real problems which lie beneath the surface issues which are dominating the conversation. What then to do with that information poses a different problem and God has another answer.

Word of wisdom: this constitutes supernatural revelation as to what action needs to be taken in a given situation, often after the word of knowledge has first been employed in order to expose the exact nature of the problem.

We need to be careful here. Sometimes we can try to give God a helping hand, albeit for the best possible reasons. What we then say ceases to be his message and becomes ours. We need the help of other Christians in order to confirm that what is said and done truly comes from God alone.

A few years ago, I spoke out in a prayer meeting a message that I felt to be from God. I suppose that I had the confidence to do so because I knew that friends were there who would test the message. Imagine my dismay, on looking up for confirmation, to see one friend shaking his head. Crestfallen, I crept over to him. 'What was wrong?' I asked. 'The first two sentences were from God; the rest was your own excellent but human assistance,' came the reply.

That check meant two things. I would not blunder on aimlessly, failing to realise what had happened and because I had the loving support of those who could discern error, I would not lose confidence. God does not want a people constantly holding back, nor does he want a people who launch out alone. Each one of us needs the correction of discerning friends.

Usually more than one person will have the same revelation. As we progress in the life of the Spirit, so our ability to hear the Lord will develop. Don't be surprised in the meantime if he gives you a helpful nudge!

Power to do

Gifts of healing: ninety per cent of the recorded ministry of Jesus on earth was devoted to healing the sick. His first instruction to his disciples when he sent them out was to 'Heal the sick' (Matt 10:8). After his death and resurrection, he performed no further healings. Now this was to be part of his commission to his disciples and we shall deal with it more fully in a later chapter.

Immediately after Pentecost, the disciples began to heal the sick, raise the dead and cast out demons. In so doing, they were only fulfilling the words of Jesus. 'I am telling you the truth: whoever believes in me will do what I do – yes, he will do even greater things' (John 14:12).

The working of miracles: while 'healing' refers to God's activity in curing physical conditions in the human body, other events come under the heading of 'miracles'. The miraculous was continually part of God's provision for the children of Israel. Miracles were a constant feature in the life of Jesus and in the experience of the early church. Prison escapes were arranged (Acts 5:17-25; 12:1-17; 16:25-40). Paul survived the bite of a deadly snake with no side effects (Acts 28:3-6). In recent years, miraculous events have been documented all over the world.

The purpose of a miracle is to meet human need and, in line with the continuing ministry of the Holy Spirit, to bring glory to Jesus. If it fulfils any other purpose, be careful, because

Satan can produce all kinds of demonic counterfeit, though he can never glorify Jesus!

The gift of faith: from the moment we are born, faith operates. When we learn to trust Jesus, we become open to that faith which the Holy Spirit produces as a fruit in our lives. However it also operates as a special gift in our lives much as Daniel experienced in the den of lions (Dan 6:17–28). In the same way, Elijah waited in full confidence for God's dramatic intervention on Mount Carmel (1 Kings 18:21; see James 5:17,18).

The 'power to do' comes from the Holy Spirit and operates in line with Scripture. God has done it all before. His Spirit is not running down in power like a battery; he is still active today.

We do need, however, to distinguish between faith and foolishness. The Holy Spirit will not just do what we demand. He brings glory to Jesus and only acts in accordance with the will of the Father. He cannot be God and live in obedience to us. If we would see God at work among us, we should not blunder into situations that angels would leave well alone nor should we be guilty of raising people's expectation of a healing or miracle, only to see their hopes dashed to the ground. It is as we ask God to lead us into his way, and confirm it with our brothers and sisters, that we can move out in confidence. What God has told us to do, that he will honour.

Power to say

The gift of tongues: this is the ability to praise God in an unknown language that may originate on earth or in heaven. We shall say more about the place of this gift in worship in a later chapter.

The gift of interpretation: this is the ability to understand what is being said when someone speaks in tongues. Without it, tongues would remain incomprehensible.

The gift of prophecy: bringing a message from God, often spontaneous, which is relevant to a particular situation. Prophecy is singled out by the Apostle Paul as a gift which we should actively seek: 'So then, my brothers, set your heart on proclaiming God's message' (1 Cor 14:39). It is not a private gift but one that should always be evaluated by the other believers present. Although prophecy can be relevant for unbelievers it has the primary function of providing 'help, encouragement, and comfort' for Christians (1 Cor 14:3).

Power to speak God's word should therefore produce powerful and direct results. Hearing God speak through ordinary people in this way should lead unbelievers to conclude, 'Truly God is here among you!' (1 Cor 14:25).

This power may operate through preaching or prayer. Prophetic praying or preaching can be a vital vehicle in God's hand when we surrender our words to his control.

These gifts and their exercise should be labelled 'handle with care'. They need to be carefully developed in the context and under the authority of the local church or fellowship. But we must not allow our recognition of the dangers inherent in their operation to prevent us from opening up ourselves to God in order that he might give us all that he wishes. As Gavin Reid concluded in the *Church of England Newspaper* some years ago, 'The plain fact of the matter is that even the best evangelical religion bears little resemblance to the experience of the Apostles. We have conditioned ourselves not to notice this ... Is there any good reason why the charismatic element in the New Testament should not continue throughout history? Should we play down evidences of a supernatural God in case they might disturb the weaker brother? Surely if God is working, we should shout it from the housetops. And if our shouting upsets the apple-cart – amen to that!'

It is as we become open to the Lord that he can give us gifts and use us. We on our part need to be sure that the glory never comes to the gift or to the recipient of the gift but to the one who is himself the giver of every good and perfect gift. Our responsibility is then to use these gifts in a way in which we build up one another and extend the ministry of the Kingdom of God.

For this reason, the apostle Peter urges that 'Each one, as a good manager of God's different gifts, must use for the good of others the special gift he has received from God. Whoever preaches must preach God's messages; whoever serves must serve with the strength that God gives, so that in all things praise may be given to God through Jesus Christ, to whom belong glory and power for ever and ever. Amen.' (1 Pet 4:10,11).

Chapter 11

Power to be witnesses

Some years ago, an American airliner, crammed full of passengers, crashed into the muddy waters of the Potomac river, just a few miles from where I live today.

Amid all the frantic rescue attempts, a helicopter arrived on the scene, trailing a rope with a lifebelt attached. Sighting an elderly man desperately clinging to some floating wreckage, the crew lowered the rope, but the man rejected it and instead of using the lifebelt himself, he chose to attach it to someone else.

Feverishly the men in the helicopter winched up the survivor and let down the line to the drowning man. Yet again, he saw another needing help and gave him the lifebelt. A third time the lifebelt was lowered – but the elderly man was gone, leaving only the wreckage floating on the surface.

This is not a bad analogy for the way in which, just about two thousand years ago, the Son of God voluntarily relinquished his life in order to serve others. By this means he gave Paradise to a dying thief, forgiveness to his failed disciple Peter, and his Spirit to his friends.

That last action was to be crucially important. It provides us with the only real explanation for the way in which 120 assorted men and women, distinguished only by an absence of theological qualifications, would soon be accused of turning their whole world upside down. These ordinary folk, who gathered together some two thousand years ago around a shared belief that a dead carpenter was actually alive, began a movement that today can claim an active worldwide membership well in excess of 1,000 million people.

No human agency could have achieved this. It lay beyond the realm of natural explanation that these events could take place. The story almost requires supernatural intervention to be believable, and that is exactly what happened. The initial dramatic growth of the Church was not achieved by military conquest or the enforced enlistment of entire people groups but through an agency none other than a convicting Spirit who was sent from Heaven in order to lead people along the road towards a genuine life-changing personal conversion.

This meant that divine intervention was absolutely necessary, and without the gift of the Holy Spirit, it could never have happened. He was to play a vital role. For when the Holy Spirit came to tired, frustrated, frightened men hiding behind locked doors, he transformed them into those who in just a few years would carry the good news of Jesus Christ throughout the length and breadth of the then known world. This was a miracle!

Jesus refused to permit his disciples to set foot outside the city limits of Jerusalem until first he had given them, in his Spirit, all the resources that they were soon to need so very desperately if they were to fulfil the great task that Jesus had entrusted into their hands. He instructed that they would be 'witnesses for me in Jerusalem, in all of Judea and Samaria and to the ends of the earth' (Acts 1:8). But first they had to wait patiently for his power. This lesson was to be an important one because the work of God cannot and must not be attempted in human strength.

As one twentieth-century prophet, A W Tozer, has reminded us: 'The popular notion that the first obligation of the Church is to spread the gospel to the uttermost parts of the earth is false. Her first obligation is to be spiritually worthy to spread it ... Had the disciples gone forth as missionaries before the day of Pentecost it would have been an overwhelming spiritual disaster, for they could have done no more than make converts after their own likeness.'

Britain is not unique as a nation where thirty-five per cent of the churches have only twenty-five or fewer members. Indeed, less than ten per cent of our churches have two hundred members or more. Many other countries have large numbers of very small churches. What is strange is that many of the younger generations have never even heard who Jesus is, yet they live in a so-called 'Christian country'.

Britain incorporates four nations where the growth of pornography, unrestricted abortion and occult practices has reached unprecedented peaks. Just about every new concept in evangelism has been tried, every new gimmick and idea, every help and resource from outside Britain has been examined – but we still fail to make a real impact on our society.

Yet Jesus has called us to be his witnesses and right now, the world is seeing the greatest move of God that has been experienced in the whole history of the Church. One Korean congregation now tops a million members – and goes on growing. In the twentieth century, Latin America witnessed a total of fifty thousand believers in 1900 rise to around 100 million by the end of that century. That kind of phenomenal growth was also paralleled in large parts of Africa. But still Western Europe seems so strangely devoid of spiritual life.

Could it be that the living God is simply waiting for us timid, frightened Christians hiding away in our cosy evangelical ghettos, praying for survival, to begin to call on him for blessing? That is why I believe that the fantastic growth of prayer groups, prayer triplets and prayer cells in the last decade is such a wonderful harbinger of all that God could still do among us. More than three hundred years ago, the great Bible commentator Matthew Henry observed the fact that 'When God intends great mercy for his people he gets them a-praying.'

When God attempts a mighty move upon a nation, he does not reserve his resources and only make them available to some kind of spiritual elite. The Lord longs to take hold of each and every one of us in order that he might make us his messengers to our dying land. 'Yes, even on my servants, both men and women, I will pour out my Spirit in those days, *and they will proclaim my message*' (Acts 2:18, emphasis mine).

It is not for us to seize the rope and rescue ourselves. Our task is always to hand on the rope to those suffering around us. It is the Holy Spirit who provides the rope. He gives us the words to say, and the authority with which to deliver them. He takes hold of insignificant, ordinary people to transform them into powerful witnesses for Jesus Christ with lives as well as words which speak the truth. It is our job to get on with the task that we have been given.

What to say?

Jesus promised that his followers would never be left unable to speak. He promised that 'When they bring you to be tried in the synagogues or before governors or rulers, do not be worried about how you will defend yourself or what you will say. For the Holy Spirit will teach you at that time what you should say' (Luke 12:11,12).

Despite that reassurance, many of us are reluctant to allow God the opportunity to speak through us. We doubt our ability and we query our intelligence or understanding. Moses had similar fears, but God's reply was straight down the line. 'Moses said ... "I am a poor speaker, slow and hesitant." The Lord quickly pointed out, "Who gives man his mouth?"' (Exod 4:10,11).

Many have started to decide on a new lifetime's ambition. They want to talk to someone about Jesus every day. They may not feel able or gifted but they are prepared to trust the Holy Spirit to use them and honour their offer of a mouth for him to use.

One Anglican bishop will occasionally become bored on a train journey. He will walk into a compartment and ask, 'Can anyone tell me who Jesus Christ really is?' As people look up, startled and embarrassed, or try to hide behind their newspapers, he will sit down to explain more fully!

Not all of us would be able to repeat his performance! I know that I so often fail to share my faith. Yet the Holy Spirit comes to our lives in order to enable us to become bolder in our faith. For the Holy Spirit is not portrayed in Scripture as one who comes to provide us with spiritual experiences designed solely for our own blessing and edification. Rather he comes to enable and empower us to meet the needs of others. He is, first and foremost, a missionary spirit, given to us so that we might fulfil the work and will of God in our lives by bringing others to Jesus.

In order to achieve this goal the Holy Spirit produced three distinctive characteristics in the lives of the early believers. He was at work in them to:

Promote compassionate actions (Acts 6:1–3)

Demonstrate spiritual power (Acts 6:8)

Generate bold proclamation (Acts 7:52)

The Holy Spirit became the energiser of the early Church in its goal of communicating the love of Jesus Christ, first to Jerusalem and subsequently to the limits of the then known world. He provided the spontaneous direction as to 'where and when' the good news should be shared. Then he generated the outstanding desire to share the faith through public preaching, demonstrative lifestyles and personal witness. He also took advantage of the everyday life situations of ordinary Christians in order to promote further opportunities for effective witness. In that way, their outreach was not a learned method or process but something that came naturally as all discovered that they were incapable of stopping themselves from 'gossiping the gospel' and sharing the truth they had found in the power of the Holy Spirit (1 Pet 1:12).

When faced with hostility, opposition, and even persecution, they found that they were not alone. They still found themselves compelled to continue to proclaim the truth of Jesus Christ and who he really is. One great example is the Apostle Paul. Despite many hazards to health and safety, he never stopped declaring the good news of Jesus Christ to all who would grant him a hearing. He always announced that his motivation was the loving compulsion that the Holy Spirit had poured into his heart (Rom 5:5; 1 Cor 9:16; 2 Cor 5:14).

This spontaneous overflow of love was not the property of Paul alone; it infected the whole of the early Church. No wonder that their growth in both quality and quantity was to be so dramatic. If further evidence is needed, then as the much-loved American sociologist and preacher Tony Campolo never tires of reminding his hearers, 'Book of Acts, baby, book of Acts!'

When considering the way in which the Holy Spirit still wants to work and speak through the people of God, one might simply observe that nothing much has changed in the course of two thousand years!

One story from the nineteenth century will serve to illustrate the point. It all began when the great American evangelist D L Moody made a promise to God, shortly after his conversion, that twenty-four hours would not pass without his sharing Jesus. One night he realised he had not kept his word. Hurrying out of bed, he feared he would meet nobody but there was a man standing under a lamp-post. He asked this perfect stranger, 'Are you a Christian?' The answer was violent rejection. The man was embarrassed, antagonistic and also extremely offended – furthermore, he said so! Finding out who Moody was, this man ensured that others told Moody in no uncertain terms the damage that he had done.

Moody was crestfallen. What a mistake! Maybe he should be less blindly enthusiastic? Now many of us could never take this course of action. But God honours the efforts of those who can, those to whom he has given that kind of opportunity and who have been imbued by the Holy Spirit with the kind of character to take advantage of it.

'Weeks passed by. One night Mr. Moody was in bed when he heard a tremendous pounding at his front door. He jumped out of bed and rushed to the door. He thought the house was on fire. He thought the man would break down the door. He opened the door and there stood this man. He said, "Mr. Moody, I have not had a good night's sleep since that night you spoke to me under the lamp-post and I have come around at this unearthly hour of the night for you to tell me what I have to do to be saved." Moody was able to lead the man to Jesus. Soon afterwards the man died and because of Moody's spiritual aggression, will spend eternity with Jesus Christ!' (R A Torrey, *Why God used D L Moody*, quoted in Calver and Delve, *God Can Use You*).

What to know?

It is only the Holy Spirit who can take us through the doubts created within our modern world and move us into the certainty of what God has for us in Jesus. 'He is the Spirit who reveals the truth about God' (John 14:17).

The Holy Spirit is the only one who is fully aware of all that Jesus really wants to say to us. So Paul affirms, 'We do not speak in words taught by human wisdom, but in words taught by the Spirit, as we explain spiritual truths to those who have the Spirit' (1 Cor 2:13). Not only does the Holy Spirit equip God's servants to teach, he also enables us to learn.

We must never lose sight of the fact that the Spirit has been given in order to lead us into all truth. While acknowledging this, we must always be careful to avoid joining the ranks of those who fail to recognise that truth is here to be lived out, not just to be believed. We must therefore be certain that we never sacrifice truth on the altar of our own limited spiritual experience and that we are never content with knowledge of the truth at the expense of experiencing that truth for ourselves. To argue that something cannot be true simply because I have never experienced it for myself, or to suggest that it is sufficient to believe something academically and never to enter into the good of that truth for myself, will usually be equally wrong. We must learn to live our truth and not be prepared to compromise it for the sake of our own convenience or comfort-zones.

How we handle the truth that God gives us is of vital importance. If we have received and come to accept a greater degree of God's truth than our neighbour, then this is not to be an occasion for self-satisfaction or self-congratulation. That would be little more than a demonstration of human pride in operation.(This section is adapted from C Calver, S Chilcraft, P Meadows, and S Gaukroger, *Shaken but not Stirred*, Spring Harvest, 1991.)

Truth and character should always live together in harmony. It is a stunning rebuke to us when those who may be less well taught than we are in their understanding of the Scriptures actually excel us in terms of love, worship and service. If that is the case then should we now reject the truth that we have come to accept? By no means, but we do need to remember that Jesus himself was 'full of grace and truth' (John 1:14). We must never be guilty of emphasising one and neglecting the other. Failure to demonstrate grace alongside truth could be as damaging as choosing to sacrifice truth in the interests of being more acceptable to others. We do need to hold tenaciously to the truth, but we can learn to disagree with others without being disagreeable ourselves. As I have come to say, living in the United States, 'We need to learn what it means to walk our talk.'

For the Holy Spirit is not content with just feeding our minds. He wants to change the way we feel as well as the way we think. We have so much in terms of conferences, books, tapes, workshops and services, all designed to impart information. More than any other country in the world, we have boundless resources to help us advance in the Christian life but so often we fail to learn because we are bogged down with doubts, guilt and fears. The constant cry is, 'How can I be sure?' As Martin Luther crisply informs us, 'The art of doubting is easy, for it is an ability that is born in us.'

Again it is the Holy Spirit who comes with a divine answer: 'I ask God from the wealth of his glory to give you power through his Spirit to be strong in your inner selves' (Eph 3:16). Not content with supplying the answers, the Holy Spirit actually brings us the faith to believe them.

The reason for this simply lies in the fact that the Holy Spirit is the supreme evangelist. He has been given to guide people towards the truth because he is himself the Spirit of truth (John 14:17; 16:3; 1 John 4:6). It is by this Spirit that people are convicted of sin. He is the author of new life and it is the Holy Spirit who brings us into the reality of being born into a new life in Jesus (John 16:7–8; 6:63; 3:6–8; 2 Cor 3:6; 1 Pet 3:18). He gives to us the assurance of knowing that our salvation has been accomplished through crucified love and that it is secure (Rom 8:16; Gal 4:6; 1 John 3:2; 4:13; 5:6).

What to do?

It is from lives that are touched by the beauty of the Holy Spirit that God can speak volumes. Witnessing for Jesus is more a matter of lifestyle than anything else. Our words should never have to be more than an explanation of our lives.

The current demand that we might be able to view the evidence before we can be expected to believe the words is beautifully illustrated in Eliza Doolittle's song from 'My Fair Lady':

Words, words, words

I'm sick of words

Sing me no song

Read me no line

Don't waste my time

Show me.

It is through the power and intervention of the Holy Spirit that we can begin to resemble Jesus. We cannot change ourselves into signposts which point away from ourselves and draw other people to him. It is only the Holy Spirit who can release us from all that we have been and start to mould us into a different likeness. '... where the Spirit of the Lord is present, there is freedom. All of us, then, reflect the glory of the Lord with uncovered faces; and that same glory, coming from the Lord, who is the Spirit, transforms us into his likeness in an ever greater degree of glory' (2 Cor 3:17,18).

The search for a different kind of living has gone on throughout the centuries. Nicodemus comes to Jesus for one reason. Although the equivalent of a Professor of Theology at the University of Jerusalem, he recognises that Jesus possesses something that he simply does not have – the power to live life as God intended. Jesus' response to him is very significant; he announces with confidence the single truth, 'That which is born of the flesh is flesh, and that which is born of the Spirit is spirit' (John 3:6, RSV).

In other words, without the Spirit, we'll never make it.

It is only by the presence of the Spirit that our lives can begin to radiate our love for Jesus and fulfil the words of Bernard of Clairveaux, 'What a man loves he will grow to look like.'

The Spirit wants to place within our lives the love and compassion of Jesus: to make us into a people who will pour out their hearts day after day for non-Christian neighbours and friends; who will learn to weep for them; who will learn how to be involved in the needs and work of the community so that bridges may be built for Jesus; who will always have an open ear to hear and a heart to love those who need help; a people who will emerge from the shadows of fearful Christian witness into a free, bold expression of the life of Jesus because his Spirit empowers us.

Some will major on words, some on acts of mercy, some on prayer, some on lifestyle but through each one the Holy Spirit will work out his divine purposes.

Jesus commissioned his disciples to go and be his witnesses in these words. 'I have been given all authority in heaven and on earth. Go, then, to all peoples everywhere and make them my disciples' (Matt 28:18,19). The reason that they could now go lay solely in the fact that Jesus possessed the authority both to send and to equip them.

That same authority applies to us as we come to Jesus confessing our inability to serve effectively apart from his strength. It is:

Our reluctance to share our faith

Our failure to pray

Our lack of love and compassion for those around us

Our isolation from our community

Our cowardice when we could have spoken

Yet into all of our failings God can insert his Spirit and when he does so, then nothing can ever be the same again. When we confess our inadequacy, when we stop trying to serve God with our human abilities, then we can plug into divine resources. Our words can be replaced by his, our life by his, our compassion by his, our prayer-life by his, and all this through the intervention within our lives of the Spirit of God himself.

D T Niles, the great Sri Lankan leader and writer, used to say that evangelism was one beggar telling another where to find bread. In other words, we might possess few resources within ourselves but it is as we allow the Holy Spirit to control our lives that he reminds us of the message and provides the resources and encouragement for its delivery. No one would pretend that such lives are easy but they are fruitful.

Perhaps, by the Spirit's help, we might even end up echoing the famous words of missionary pioneer C T Studd when he announced, 'O let us not rust out – let us not glide through the world and then slip quietly out, without having even blown the trumpets loud and long for our blessed Redeemer. At the very least let us see to it that the Devil holds a thanksgiving service in hell when he gets the news of our departure from the field of battle.'

Chapter 12

The Holy Spirit
and the Church

Sometimes we become so excited with the fact that the Holy Spirit arrives to make his home within our individual lives that we forget that he also comes to introduce us into the privilege of becoming a part of a whole new family. In other words, we fail to recognise that this same Holy Spirit acted as the midwife involved in bringing to birth the Church of Jesus Christ. Not only does the Spirit bring to our lives the joys of personal salvation, he also introduces us into the realities of becoming part of this whole new alternative society.

It is the Holy Spirit who acts as the guarantee that we now belong to this family that will be together forever. The plain and simple truth is that a point in history will eventually arrive when the Lord Jesus will return to marry us – his Church. One day we will begin to rule together with King Jesus in a reign that will last throughout eternity. Until that time arrives, we are called upon to remain here in order that we may act as the hands and feet of Jesus, his agents upon this planet, preparing for his return.

It is for this reason that the Holy Spirit has been given to us to act as our helper. Because of the aid and intervention of the Holy Spirit the good news about Jesus would be taken to the whole world, and many in the world, over the centuries, would be brought to Jesus (John 14:17–26; 16:13). This was vividly demonstrated on the Day of Pentecost. The new believers received the Holy Spirit at the moment of their conversion, they were immediately added by the Holy Spirit to the infant Church, began to share in its life and practices and gave testimony to their new-found faith. The process then continued with the next batch of new believers and so the Church grew.

The Holy Spirit was constantly active in empowering this new community for Jesus by equipping the Church for its ministry. It is scarcely surprising that this became such a major priority in the work of the Holy Spirit. He was not given merely to bless us but to make us a blessing to others. He did not come to deal with us just as individuals but as part of a corporate whole. He was not concerned solely for the present needs but to prepare us for eternity. In all of this, his desire was to fulfil the intentions of Jesus because the heart of Jesus was for his Church.

But why is the Church so important?

The simple fact is that, time and again, Jesus spoke and acted in order to gain a people for himself who would be his love-gift to his Father. Their unity would then illustrate his own oneness with the Father and the Son. Their compassion was going to demonstrate his own commitment to the poor and the dispossessed. Their own lifestyle was intended to reveal the manner in which his Holy Spirit took hold of ordinary people and transformed their lives. Their witness would be the very means by which so many others would be brought to Jesus.

The conclusion is obvious: 'church' has always resided right at the very heart of the intentions of Jesus for this world.

Many of us may find areas of church life boring or difficult. It is good, therefore, to see this from the perspective of Jesus because things can be wrong or awry in a local church yet it remains the body of believers for whom Jesus died. But Church does not constitute an unwanted extra imposed upon our Christian understanding. Instead it lies at the very central core of all that Jesus determined and lived and died to achieve. He had clearly revealed his intentions when he boldly proclaimed, 'I will build my church, and the gates of Hades will not overcome it' (Matt 16:18). This is the problem that so many of us have to face up to when confronted by negative views of church, either from others or from ourselves! For Jesus specifically brought his Church into existence. He ordained it, he commissioned it and he intends that it should be the express revelation of his glory.

We were designed to be his Church. This is something that we can never achieve separately but only together. The simple fact is that the Christian faith is inescapably corporate. Scripture points to this one people of God as 'the Church'. The amazing truth is that this international family is what Jesus died to bring about. There is a great equalising truth, and it is that whatever our race, class, education, gender, background or country of origin, we are all sinners for whom Jesus Christ has died (Rom 3:23; 8:32). Now we are to live as those for whom he has a great and wonderful purpose.

We are to receive his new life and learn to be so many things. Because we are now part of the Church, the Holy Spirit is able to work upon our lives in order that we might become the servants (1 Pet 2:16); children (John 1:12); ambassadors (2 Cor 5:20); witnesses (Acts 1:8); and even the friends (John 15:15) of Jesus.

Each of these descriptions was placed in its plural form so that we could be left in no doubt that, as Christians, we only qualify to fit into these categories by our association with our brothers and sisters in Christ. We have all become believers, not as the result of any good deeds we have performed but simply through the grace and kindness of crucified love. This has been true for each and every one of us. We are therefore 'all one in union with Christ Jesus' (Gal 3:28).

We were created and prepared to be his Church. This is something that we can never achieve separately but only together. The simple fact is that the Christian faith is inescapably corporate. So we know that the Holy Spirit unites us all through our shared relationship in Jesus. That is why we are now part of the same family – we are brothers and sisters in Jesus Christ.

Unlikely as it may seem, we really were made for one another!

This principle is plainly revealed in Scripture and formed the basis of the heart-cry of Jesus to his Father in John 17. Four times he pleaded with his Father on behalf of his disciples and those who would follow them that 'they might be one.' The repetition only serves to reinforce how important this was to Jesus. He longed that we might know what it means to love and support each other. This was not just because he thought that it would be a good way to ensure the survival of the Church but also because it fell directly in line with the will of his Father.

It would be true to say that 'Church' constitutes a clear demonstration of God's love. He has not left us to struggle through on our own but has given us a family. Nor is this family just intended to shore up our defenses and ensure our survival. It lies at the very core of God's action plan. Put simply, the Church lies right at the heart of his eternal purpose. It would be true to say that where God intends to act within the world, he is going to do so through his Church.

But where is the Church?

Let us hope most of us have outgrown the misconception that 'Church' refers to a gothic-style building located on a neighbouring street corner. Moving on into a recognition that the Church refers to people, rather than to bricks and mortar, certainly represents a degree of progress. However, for too many of us, our understanding remains locked into a view of 'Church' that is confined to the fellowship we receive in our own locality. In other words, we have got through to the local church but believe that the universal Church is a concept reserved for eternity!

Too often we have fallen into the trap of making the bride of Christ too small.

It is the variety of this family that is truly astonishing. Its members are drawn not only from every kindred, tribe and nation but also from every class, culture and generation. It clearly must have required the express design and purpose of the living God to bring such a disparate and unlikely group together in order to live as his people. Yet we often are content to live in total ignorance of the needs and situations that are today confronting the vast majority of our spiritual brothers and sisters.

One definition of the Church is that it is 'the community of all those in whom the Holy Spirit dwells'. In other words, it consists of all those who have the Spirit (Rom 8:14–16). The true universal Church therefore embraces all those who are children of God because we share the same Heavenly Father (1 Cor 12:13; Eph 4:4).

If we were to be content to live on earth with a bride who was fractured and disjointed by national or ethnic distinctions, then the day of our Lord's return could present a picture of his arriving at the altar in order to marry his bride only to be greeted by an arm rolling up the aisle, closely followed by a leg, then a couple of fingers, hotly pursued by an ear, or some other section of the anatomy! Imagine the confusion as all the various parts desperately tried to join themselves together into a bride that would be fit and appropriate for a King!

Sometimes I get the feeling that those of us who are part of Jesus' Church in the United Kingdom might believe that we are the torso and that everyone on that day will have to fit in around us. This is all such a tragic misrepresentation of what that time will really be like. It will be a day of glad celebration when we realise that our common family bond in Jesus transcends any distinction of gender, social standing, racial distinction or even nationality.

In fact, there won't be any British Christians in heaven. Nor will there be any African ones or North American or Asian Christians. There will only be family. It would be good if none of us were faced with having to apologise for a neglect of churches and family members other than those in our own country. This must be especially true when we have been entrusted with an abundance of those resources which others have needed so desperately. How much more true if our failure to recognise their need had turned out to be a matter of life and death!

It would be far better if our gathering together in Heaven were to be a time of mutual thanksgiving and gratitude, so good if we could celebrate the way in which we had shared, prayed and supported each other because of our shared relationship in Jesus. It is really difficult to imagine the look or the words which the one who told the story of the Good

Samaritan would have for those of us who by simple ignorance or neglect had allowed our brothers and sisters to die.

Some people would be offended if I were to suggest that conditions in Southern Sudan are reminiscent of a bygone age in the rest of the world yet that assessment would be true. A country which is approximately the size of Western Europe possesses only ten miles of paved roads.

The first time I arrived at the remote village of Leithnomh, I was greeted by one or two inquisitive onlookers as our little plane bounced unhappily along an apology for an airstrip. To call it a runway would involve stretching human credulity beyond acceptable limits.

It was not only the landing strip that was primitive; the village and its population were clearly suffering, and many exhibited a whole host of symptoms related to chronic malnutrition and serious deprivation. The first problem was that we were not expected. It was the middle of a period of such extreme famine that the vast majority of the people were simply concentrating on the need to survive.

Walking through the village, I noticed that about two hundred people had gathered together and were sitting on the ground underneath a spreading tree. Now anyone who knows Africa will appreciate that this usually indicates a religious meeting. Being inquisitive, I paused to ask the people what they were doing. The reply was instantaneous.

'We're worshipping Jesus.'

Then came their immediate question to me, 'Have you ever heard of him?'

No sooner had I replied that I had, when the further enquiry came, 'We've heard that there is a book; you haven't ever seen one, have you?'

Before we were allowed to conduct a food assessment or look together at ways in which we could begin to meet the physical needs of these people who were just about surviving in a state of semi-starvation, we first had to respond to their insistence that we provide them with Bibles.

Therefore it is perhaps no great surprise to record that a few months later over one thousand people from that village and the surrounding area were baptised.

After the building of a school, the provision of initial veterinary services, the beginnings of the training of lay-leaders for the emerging church and the construction of a mini-hospital, that village was systematically and regularly bombed over a period of several weeks by the air force of the Islamic fundamentalist Northern Sudanese Government in Khartoum. The prime targets were the church and the World Relief compound.

In another part of Southern Sudan, the villages in the area of South Bor witnessed the sudden conversion of over ninety per cent of the population in a period of just a few weeks. As in Leithnomh, it has proved difficult to discover any agent of direct human involvement in the process. As far as one can learn, there was no visiting evangelist nor did those areas possess a single church or local pastor. The absence of a missionary or evangelistic initiative should not serve to make us sceptical as to the effectiveness of this work. The annals of church history are riddled with illustrations of times when the Holy Spirit has chosen suddenly and sovereignly to intervene in human affairs.

Many have commented that what is taking place today in Southern Sudan is reminiscent of the way in which the Spirit of God chose to take action at certain times of human desperation during the nineteenth and early twentieth centuries. These new 'baby' Christians may well be spiritually immature and largely ignorant of Scripture but this is scarcely surprising in the light of the almost total absence of pastors or trained leaders. What is needed is food, medicine, Bibles, support and encouragement to know that the rest of the family has not forgotten them!

It is certainly true that God is not dependent on us. However, over recent years I have become more and more convinced that I had allowed my own faith to become far too narrow, limited and parochial. I have had to repent for my own rejection of the way that God was actively moving in so many areas outside the United Kingdom. It was not that I was hostile to my brothers and sisters overseas or to initiatives taken on their behalf. It was just that I did not view this as my own concern. I was wrong.

Wherever God is at work in this world, he does require us to pay attention! His activity will never be limited in any way by either our acquiescence, approval or direct involvement. But we can be absolutely certain that he would not be happy to discover that his people were seeking either to hamper, reject or pay no attention to what his Spirit is doing. Whether this comes from neglect or antipathy is not the issue, for the results, in terms of the unmet need of our brothers and sisters, remain exactly the same.

But why is the Church here?

For many of my generation, there has emerged a real need to recognise a desire for a sense of 'cultural relevance' in the churches. It is all very well to recognise that an individual life has encountered Jesus but what about the institution to which one then belongs? Is it able to be relevant and important to life in the real world today?

The idea of total separation from the wider world emerged in many twentieth century evangelical churches. This resulted in a whole gamut of changes, so that instead of Christian maturity being measured by the impact the life of an individual had on the rest of society, it came to be viewed in terms of the degree to which one succeeded in withdrawing from direct contact with the rest of society. It was almost as if involvement in the local community would inevitably result in our being contaminated by it. Far from light exterminating darkness, it was as if the Church had come to a fearful belief that darkness could extinguish the light.

If this were true at a local level, it became even more obvious in relation to international matters. What would appear to be vital issues such as global poverty, economic exploitation or human rights seemed to be regarded as vaguely 'unspiritual'. These were more to be regarded as areas of concern for the rest of society, rather too 'worldly' for the Church to become more intimately involved. It was almost as if evangelicals felt that they could become contaminated if they moved beyond the safety of their own comfort-zone.

Some felt that too great an involvement in social issues could result in Christians being diverted from their real task of preaching the gospel yet often it was their very own brothers and sisters around the world who were being condemned by their neglect to be the victims of starvation, persecution, slavery or injustice. This could be individual oppression or related to the society or community of which they were a part. Either way, one gained the impression that many evangelicals were rather proud of the fact that these areas of concern should be consigned to more liberal churches. It may sound harsh, but evangelical Christians only gave the impression of being busy constructing ghettos from their own church activities where they could feel safe, secure and unchallenged. For so-called Bible-believing churches the sphere of social, community and political involvement had largely become a no-go area.

During the 1970s, a new congregation, which called itself the Invisible Church, was planted in London. I had the opportunity of preaching there on a couple of occasions. They were a great bunch of people but I must confess to having a little difficulty with the name they had chosen for themselves. Of course, there is truth in the fact that all committed Christians are part of a vast corporate body of believers that will only be finally revealed on that glorious day when Jesus returns to take his people to reign with him for eternity. In that sense, we are certainly part of an invisible Church yet while we are here on earth, our role is very different.

Jesus told his disciples that they were to be 'the light of the world'. He instructed them to 'let your light so shine before men, that they may see your good deeds and praise your Father in heaven' (Matt: 5;14–16). He pointed out that lamps are designed not to be concealed but to be placed on open public display where they can fulfil the function for which they were intended. In exactly the same way, we are called to shine out as lights in our world, in order that others may also be attracted to Jesus. So to speak of ourselves as 'the invisible Church' would, in this sense, really be a contradiction in terms!

For this reason, we need to be careful about the way in which we understand our evangelical concern for separation from the world. Clearly there are habits, activities and even friendships or pastimes where the Holy Spirit will call a halt to our previous practices and allegiances. In answering the question, 'What would Jesus do?' we will be forced to concede the answer 'not this' and allow him to enable us to change our ways.

While it is certainly right to affirm that we are not called to be 'of' the world, it is also undoubtedly true that we are called to remain 'in' it. Jesus continually enraged the religious establishment of his day by his insistence on spending time with the most unsavoury members of society. In fact, Jesus appears never to have been very fussy about the initial character of those he spent time with. The reason was that he had not come to reinforce the old religious habits of his age. Instead, he came to bring about in the lives of individuals a revolution of love which would usher in the birth of a whole new society on earth. Jesus had come to build his Church.

Someone once observed this concerning the carpenter from Nazareth: 'All the armies that ever marched and all the navies that ever sailed and all the parliaments that ever sat and all the kings that ever reigned, put together, have not affected the life of man upon earth as has that one solitary life.'

So our responsibility is not simply to survive here in order that one day we may enjoy the privileges of Heaven. Once we have discovered the impact of Jesus on ourselves we have no right to want to keep him to ourselves. Our God-given task is to go and reveal his love to those who have yet to meet him. Now this is easy to say but much harder to put into practice.

Most of us would prefer a faith that simply demanded our attendance at a continuous litany of meetings, the performance of a regular devotional routine and the avoidance of extreme immoral practices. But this is not what it means to be a disciple of Jesus. He never gave us the right simply to add Bible-reading, praying, churchgoing and missing out on a whole string of 'do nots' to our old lifestyle. Instead the implications of becoming a Christ-follower were to be far more radical. The standards were beyond mere human abilities and that is why the Holy Spirit has been given to us. Not just so that we might be happy, or even just holy, but to make us useful as well.

But what should the Church be doing?

Above all, we were called to make a difference in this world. For this reason the Spirit has come to make us to be salt and light within our society. These are the twin demands that Jesus lays upon all of us (Matt 6:13-16). He does not give us the right to choose between them for the two are inextricably intertwined in God's purposes for his people. If, by his grace, we are to change our world, then we are not at liberty just to choose the one that appeals the most to us and ignore the other. Biblically, the two come as a combined package, for evangelistic proclamation and social demonstration are not to be divorced from each other.

It is interesting to note that salt precedes light, for that is often God's way. Salt acts as a fertiliser and detergent, it prepares the way for the light that is given to achieve two things - both to produce a division between light and darkness and to conquer the darkness. John affirms that this is because darkness can never 'understand' (a better translation is 'master') the light that comes from God (John 1:5). But then, because the light is at work, it will illuminate still further areas that require cleansing and change.

To have social action without the gospel would create little more than the puny efforts of secular humanism. Take that the other way round and one is too often left with the barren emptiness of words without deeds. In the Sermon on the Mount, Jesus uniquely teaches the significance of both, and the strategic importance of their standing together. We must be very careful never to allow our own prejudices, traditions or preferences to take precedence over the Master's instructions.

It is important to note the way that Mary's song, the Magnificat, associates the spiritually poor and the spiritually hungry with each other. The hungry and thirsty whom God satisfies are those who 'hunger and thirst for righteousness.' Such spiritual hunger and thirst is a characteristic of all God's people because our ultimate desires are spiritual and not material. While pagans are engrossed in the pursuit of possessions Christians are truly to be different. For our quest is for God's kingdom and righteousness; that is what we are instructed to 'seek first' (Matt 6:33).

This righteousness is to have a two-fold application. First, it is to be moral, in that our lives are to display a character and a conduct that pleases God. Jesus' instructions concerning our response to such issues as murder, reconciliation, legal action, adultery, divorce and remarriage, oaths, revenge and hatred of our enemies (Matt 5:21–48) now go way beyond the Old Testament requirements. It is not only in deed that our righteousness must be worked out but also in thought as well.

But it would be wrong to assume that we can confine our righteousness merely to the level of being a private and personal affair. Biblical righteousness must always include social righteousness as well. This involves our becoming concerned about our integrity in business dealings and family affairs, standing with those facing personal victimisation, combatting injustice both at home and abroad, defending those who are weak and vulnerable, giving support to the disadvantaged and seeking to bring freedom to the victims of oppression. In these ways, Christians are committed to hunger for righteousness in the whole community as something that is pleasing to a righteous God.

The Holy Spirit is always seeking to bring transforming change and renewal into the life of the local church. Sometimes we are guilty of falling into a tempting trap. We view this desire as simply relating to the provision for us of the latest spiritual experience that has been thoughtfully designed for our enjoyment. To relegate the Holy Spirit's activities in the life of the church to this selfish level, or to reduce his ministry among the people of God to solely this type of activity, is to make a tragic mistake.

So what are the Holy Spirit's ambitions for the local church? If we really are serious in wanting to know the answer to this question, then there is much that we can learn from our brothers and sisters around the world, but supremely we must examine what Scripture has to say on the subject. There again we should need not only to review what instruction it gives but also be prepared to learn for ourselves from the models that it provides.

It almost goes without saying that we would not go far wrong if we simply sought to follow the model of the Jerusalem church. It certainly represents an early effective model of what the Church ought to look like and we must surely also ask whether this is what the Holy Spirit would want us to resemble? For members of this local church were less preoccupied with the personal blessings they received, many as they were, than with other things. They wanted to be:

Staying free from social discrimination – the church seems to have included people who were drawn from all strata of society. Gentiles were missing, but in Jerusalem itself this was hardly surprising, and this issue awaited resolution at the later Jerusalem Council. The rich, the poor, and the middle-classes all worshipped together. Mary owned a large house (Acts 12:12-17); Barnabas and Simon of Cyrene, along with Ananias and Sapphira, were all property owners. But the church also included widows, beggars and those from the lower classes who were sick. Many were clearly middle-class, and while it may be popular to consider that all fishermen must automatically have been poor, Zebedee, the father of James and John was sufficiently well-off to have employed other workers in the family fishing business. While these social distinctions are clearly there they seem to have been of little significance to these early believers. This is only as it should be, for James was to write that in Christ the poor are rich in faith (James 2:5).

Demonstrating their concern for each other – not only was discrimination absent but the believers learned what it meant to share their material possessions with one another.

Spreading the good news of the Kingdom – this Christian community was a large church from the outset, but it represented a good example of an integrated approach to mission. Open air preaching, personal witness, and faith under fire all combined to provide a powerful explanation of the lifestyle they lived and the Jesus they served. All Jerusalem was soon aware of what was happening (Acts 5:28).

Caring for the poor – all Jews accepted the need as part of their faith to demonstrate compassion and share their resources with the poor. But evidently in the first century this was not happening as it should. By caring so well for the poor the Jerusalem church demonstrated exactly how it could be done. Their involvement included care for widows and orphans, the appointment of some of their leaders to special responsibilities involved in the administration of social programmes, healing the sick, voluntarily surrendering property, common meals, shared housing and a variety of forms of direct evangelism. Because the area immediately to the south of the Temple was a poor district, the fact of their consistent preaching in that specific locality may have been a conscious way of showing their desire to make the gospel especially accessible to the most disadvantaged members of the community. There was also daily distribution of food. Luke's verdict on their efforts was that 'there were no needy persons among them' (Acts 4:34).

Jesus had preached and demonstrated justice for the poor. It is significant that the early Christians were obedient to Christ's demands. Already the Jerusalem Church as a community was putting his principles into practice. It is not therefore surprising to note that a concern for the poor remained a hallmark of the early Christians (Acts 9:36; 10:4; James 1:27 – 2:4). But God never forgets the generosity of his people. It was all going to come home to them. When famine came, Paul organised emergency relief. Those who had given so generously would now receive (Rom 15:25–27; Gal 2:10).

I wonder if you feel as uncomfortable as I do when confronted with this model? Too often we prove to be guilty of confining the operations of the Holy Spirit to the cosy, privatised area of me, my church and Jesus. Actually he wants to do something far more radical. He wants to take what he has done in renewing both our individual and church lives and use this as a launching pad to lead his Church back to the adventure of both challenging and transforming our world.

It is a sobering question to face up to honestly, but if the lifestyle of the Jerusalem church represents the kind of thing the Holy Spirit does in the life of a local church, then how would we rate ourselves? On the basis of the evidence that is provided by our lives within our own community, both individually and corporately, can we be sure that he is alive and well and operating freely out of your church - and mine? Or have we also stopped short, stuck somewhere between the realities of Calvary and a genuine Pentecost?

Chapter 13

True worship

Looking down from the platform, I could see a wonderful thing happening among the congregation below. Just row after row of Christians praising God, each one comfortable as they worshipped in the way that came most naturally to them but all choosing to express their worship in different ways from others around them.

For so long, we have been processed into the 'right' way to do things. Consequently, we have been conditioned into all doing the same thing at the same time; uniformity has been the order of the day. But on this occasion, my eyes strayed along a row to see all the glorious variety of Christians in worship, each accepting the others, differences included! One had his arms straight up in the air, while his neighbour's hands were firmly at her sides. Next to them stood a married couple, the husband with his hands outstretched at hip height, his wife with hers grasping their song sheet. Another man had his hands in his pockets, while his wife danced up the aisle! All were worshipping God in their own way. Some offered their hearts and lives to the Lord in a quiet meditative fashion; others expressed their sense of joy and gratitude with total abandon!

Since that first time, I have rarely visited a meeting of Christians in the United Kingdom where that variety is not evident. Each is comfortable in offering to God her own worship, refusing to be thrust into the straightjacket of copying her neighbours. The miracle lies in the fact that, in the main, no one is dismissing his brother or sister as being either over-emotional or too traditional. A quiet spirit of mutual appreciation is beginning to release us from the sense that we all have to conform to the same style of worship, and that is a miracle in itself. Whether in new or old churches, established or independent churches, youth or traditional churches, we have begun to allow one another to be who we are in Jesus.

The great thing about our variety of church traditions and denominations is that we can choose the one in which we can feel most comfortable, but we must never do so with an attitude which is contemptuous of those who choose to worship in a different way. No cultural objection should influence our attitudes to worship. If actions and words conform to Scriptural standards, they can and will please God, even if they are different from our own usual and accepted form of worship.

Communicating the concept of worship

'Worship' is one of the great words of the church. Unfortunately, it is also one of the most misunderstood. Words can easily be misleading and a word regularly used can prove the old adage that 'familiarity breeds contempt'. For example, the more we talk about Sunday morning worship, the easier it is to equate 'worship' with our church activities preceding the sermon! Now these may well be worshipful but they can never be said to present a complete picture of Christian worship.

Presbyterians posed one of the key questions of Church history when they asked, 'What is the chief end (ie purpose) of man?' Their own answer was one that is echoed by Scriptures, apostles, prophets and saints since the world began: 'to glorify God and to enjoy him for ever.' To worship God is to fulfil the whole purpose of his creation. He made us to worship him!

Rather than attempting yet another definition of the word 'worship', let us take a moment or two to examine all those facets which are included in this glorious concept.

Worship involves expressing God's great 'worthship'. In the same way that lovers whisper to each other their true feelings, so we worship God when we tell him how much we feel that he is worth – to us!

This can never be a cold, impersonal statement. For too long, our worship has tended to be confined to a rigid process or ritual. But what is really demanded of worship is that we 'feel in the heart'. Unimpassioned worship is impossible. To participate in worship means to resign as a spectator and get involved in honestly expressing to God our love for him.

Worship must therefore be an expression, given back to God, of what he is to us! In some appropriate manner, be it singing, prayer, reading of Scripture, meditation or some other means, we will express 'a humbling but delightful sense of admiring awe and astonished wonder.'

This can only happen when we've stopped trying to stand before God and speak our own wisdom. Worship is for those who are being humbled into a true understanding of themselves as creatures before a Creator. Only then can come the giving of time, silence and wonder, in admiration and awe before the living God. As Jesus said, 'I will show you whom to fear; fear God' (Luke 12:5).

Worship incorporates the praise of a grateful people, joyfully acknowledging all that God has given us.

It took the words of a twentieth century evangelical prophet to help me realise just how crucial this issue really is. As A W Tozer observed, 'Without worship we go about miserable ... the purpose of God in sending his Son to die and rise and live and be at the right hand of God the Father was that he might restore to us the missing jewel, the jewel of worship; that we might come back and learn to do again that which we were created to do in the first place – worship the Lord in the beauty of holiness, to spend our time in awesome wonder and adoration of God, feeling and expressing it, letting it get into our labours and doing nothing except as an act of worship to Almighty God through his Son Jesus Christ. I say that the greatest tragedy in the world today is that God has made man in his image and made him to worship him, made him to play the harp of worship before the face of God day and night, but he has failed God and dropped the harp. It lies voiceless at his feet' (*Worship, the Missing Jewel of the Evangelical Church*).

Enjoying the practice of worship

How can we as creatures, and sinful ones at that, properly worship our Creator? Here, as in all things, God himself has taken the initiative for us. When Adam sinned, he didn't go looking for God but God came seeking him. When mankind had lost the ability to worship God, the Lord restored that gift through his Holy Spirit. 'Be filled with the Spirit. Speak to one another with the words of psalms, hymns, and sacred songs; sing hymns and psalms to the Lord with praise in your hearts' (Eph 5:18–19). One purpose of our being filled with the Spirit is to enable us to encourage each other in our worship of the Lord.

Of course, we can worship God while alone but it is a practice which we develop together, not apart. That is why Paul instructs the Ephesians to sing to each other. It is as we support one another that our natural function as creatures worshipping our Creator can be re-established. It is the Holy Spirit who gives to us that continuous daily refreshing from God to enable us not just to praise God, but also to encourage that same spirit of worship in each other. The net result is summarised by the Psalmist in the concept that God is then enthroned on the praises of his people. In other words, as God gives us the strength, so we give him the honour and acclaim which is his due.

In corporate worship: not just going through the motions of a well-established routine but bringing a specific offering from our own hearts to the Lord. It is becoming ever more important for a local church or fellowship to give the opportunity for members of the body to bring their own contributions to acts of corporate worship. The other side of the coin is that we must then be prepared to receive either encouragement and endorsement, or gentle guidance and help (or even rebuke) if we have gone wrong! Such gentle discipline creates the atmosphere of security and support in which each member of the body can continue and deepen his worship and relationship with the Lord. Whether it is a prayer, a song, a reading, a hymn or a word from the Lord, we all have a contribution to make.

In meditation: just taking a phrase of Scripture and seeking to reflect upon its truth. For example, 'Those who have the Son have life' (1 John 5:12, NIV). In our frenetically busy world, it can be incredibly therapeutic simply to take time – on the bus, at the kitchen sink, during lunch – and allow those words to minister the truth of God's word to you. Digest them – and worship him! It may be just a phrase of Scripture which spoke to you in your own prayer and Bible reading, but the Holy Spirit applies it to your spirit to generate genuine worship.

In praise and prayer: the worship of a grateful heart is expressed in thanksgiving to God for all that he has given to us. Only a few years ago, such praise would have been expressed in a very subdued fashion. Such quiet gratitude voiced in simple prayer is still the means for many to express their praise. However, other forms of expression have also become the norm in a wide variety of churches. Over the last thirty years, a whole new vocabulary of worship has emerged. This employs modern music to accompany songs which are often based on the words of Scripture but are less formal than traditional hymns. These provide a genuine means of encouraging one another to corporate thanksgiving, while operating to a different rhythm from that which dominated evangelical worship for some hundreds of years.

New styles of worship have also acquired new prominence. There has been a rediscovery of the biblical understanding that our bodies can be used in worship. Dance, either in specially choreographed sequences or as a spontaneous expression of praise to God, has opened new dimensions for some, while others have found that the lifting of hands to the Lord is a helpful expression of devotion and gratitude.

Through spiritual gifts: In hundreds of churches drawn from a variety of different denominations, the use of spiritual gifts has acquired a new prominence. In such churches the regular use of the gift of tongues, with accompanying interpretation as outlined in 1 Corinthians 14 by the Apostle Paul, has become a significant means of stimulating communal worship of God. Other gifts such as prophecy, words of knowledge and encouragement, alongside various other gifts of ministry, have also taken their place in corporate worship. Healing services have become a regular feature in the most unlikely church situations. This same pattern is also witnessed in the style of worship.

Within a relatively brief period of time, new patterns of worship have emerged and have gained broad acceptance within a variety of evangelical churches. It is often entertaining to witness the reaction of visiting preachers from overseas who have not previously conducted meetings in this country when they are suddenly faced with the unexpected sight of around one-third of their congregation raising their hands before the Lord. It is too easy an answer to suggest that the British Church has gone 'charismatic'! Yet many who raise their hands would be appalled at that suggestion!

We are currently experiencing a reaction against the years when traditionally conservative British evangelical Christians were nicknamed 'God's frozen chosen'!

Many in society have raised a clenched fist to God, illustrating their agreement to the words that Jesus prophetically used, 'We don't want this man to be our king' (Luke 19:14). In a visually parallel response, many Christians are showing their own reaction to this rejection. They choose to demonstrate, through raising their hands in the air during times of worship, the complete submission to the will of Jesus which they want in their lives.

Avoiding the pitfalls of worship

As with every good thing, there are hazards we must be careful to avoid. The growth of free expression in worship can easily lead to dangers. If these are not avoided, Satan can succeed in directing large numbers of the people of God up a spiritual cul-de-sac from which they will not easily escape.

Over-enthusiasm: I once found myself sitting on the platform at a meeting while a woman gaily danced up the aisle. A few moments later, another followed suit. I turned to my neighbour to check that he felt as I did. One woman was allowing her love for the Lord to be expressed naturally through her dance, while the other looked suspiciously as if she was trying to draw attention to herself. We need to watch our motives and to remember Paul's gentle words of censure. 'Everything must be done in a proper and orderly way' (1 Cor 14:39–40).

Spiritual superiority: When I was at school, a boy's worth was measured by the number of wins his conker achieved! Sometimes I am aware today of situations where spiritual worth is measured by whether or not one speaks in tongues, raises hands or dances! Such attitudes are dangerously immature.

Paul prefaces his instructions to behave correctly with these words: 'Be eager to prophesy; and do not forbid speaking in tongues' (1 Cor 14:39, NIV). Yet nowhere in Scripture is there any teaching that those who do not speak in tongues are spiritually second-class citizens!

The purpose of this gift is to enable us to praise God when we run out of words. Often we can share with the Lord all that we feel about him only to discover that we are speechless with wonder in worshipping him – so he simply provides new words to add to our praise.

Many are confused as to how we receive this gift. We should be careful to avoid any special methods or techniques – they are unbiblical and can be dangerous. Some years ago I found myself talking to a Christian businessman from a charismatic evangelical church. He longed to praise God in tongues but had never felt free to do so. I pointed out that if he wanted to talk to a non-Christian about Jesus, he would hardly ask the Lord for the words, open his mouth and stand there awkwardly, gaping open-mouthed at the non-Christian waiting for something to come! He would speak out, and so it is with the gift of tongues. I felt that I had done nothing other than help him to get over the 'making it so supernaturally complicated' barrier – yet he went home praising God!

Tongues may also be used in public worship. Here Paul insists that interpretation must follow, otherwise, 'How will anyone understand what you are talking about if your message given in strange tongues is not clear ... The person who speaks in strange tongues, then, must pray for the gift to explain what is said' (1 Cor 14:9,13). Because a tongue is an expression of praise to God, the interpretation will usually similarly reflect the praise of a worshipping heart.

Some of us are quite satisfied praising God in our own language. Others appropriate the gift of tongues and find that it enables them to express the devotion of their hearts to the Lord. Paul encourages the Corinthians to hold in balance their use of this gift of praying in the Spirit with praying in the mind. He insists that both are fruitful and that the former is not superior to the latter or vice versa.

Paul's deepest concern is expressed thus: 'Since you are eager to have the gifts of the Spirit, you must try above everything else to make greater use of those which help to build up the church' (1 Cor 14:12).

Self-centredness: On the one hand we can become too immersed in fulfilling our own desires; on the other we can be too concerned with what others are doing.

In the latter case, we concentrate so much on the actions and attitudes of those around us that we can easily become guilty of neglecting the one who is the true focus of our worship. The same danger applies to the former situation where things that are good in themselves can be carried to an unfortunate extreme. It is possible to over-emphasise our freedom in worship to the detriment of other important things.

A friend recently went away on a special weekend retreat where a great deal of time and emphasis was spent on movement and dance. These exercises in 'spiritual aerobics' were good in themselves but took so much time that no mention was made during the whole weekend of how, as Christians, we could minister to our hurt society or be involved in real evangelism.

This is especially true in the area of spiritual gifts. It is possible to recover a necessary emphasis on the Spirit's present-day ministry among us at the expense of paying proper attention to his eternal character. If we are not careful, we find ourselves concentrating too much on our own sense of spiritual excitement rather than what God wants to do through our lives. The result is that we can find ourselves emphasising the gifts and neglecting the Giver!

It is very easy to become so committed to worship that we become totally self-indulgent. We fail to realise that God is after neither our worship nor our service in isolation one from the other. He longs to create a cycle in which, having expressed our love for him, we then long to share that good news with others. Their response will, in turn, provide further reason for our expression of gratitude to God.

Worship
(Sharing our love with God)

Praise   Service
(Sharing our gratitude)   (Sharing love with others)

Witness
(Sharing the good news)

Where our emphasis is always on service, we tend to revert to good deeds out of duty rather than as a free expression of love to God. But where our concerns are confined to worship meetings we tend not only to add to the already over-full Christian calendar but also to concentrate on satisfying our own needs while blindly ignoring a dying world.

If our expression of worship to God is to be an acknowledgement of his 'worthship', recognising his position in relation to us, then we must do what he tells us. It is not enough to offer lip service to a living God; he requires actions as well. There are moments in each of our lives when we need to remember the words that were spoken by the prophet Samuel to a disobedient king. He asked Saul a simple question, and then delivered a swingeing rebuke: 'Which does the Lord prefer: obedience or offerings and sacrifices? It is better to obey him than to sacrifice ...' (1 Sam 15:22).

It is never enough to sit on the fence enjoying our own worship nor is it right to spend our time passing judgement on the different styles of worship among us. Instead, we must bring to the one who gave us everything the offering of our lips and our lives. In other words, we worship God both in what we say and in how we live. Let us spend less of our time in examining the worship of others, and more on asking whether our own is acceptable to God.

'So then, my brothers, because of God's great mercy to us I appeal to you: Offer yourselves as a living sacrifice to God, dedicated to his service and pleasing to him. This is the true worship that you should offer' (Rom 12:1).

Chapter 14

Living by the Spirit

One minor league football club became a bit of a joke. At one stage in a particularly disastrous season, it had half a dozen fixtures left and still hadn't won a game! The problem was that losing had grown to be so familiar and players had become so accustomed to failure that winning might have constituted a problem!

That same sense of failure can often result in our crashing down in our Christian lives. Time and again we act in good faith, responding to calls for a deeper commitment, only to fail and fail again. Promises, resolutions, good intentions – all seem to be to no avail.

Actress Glenda Jackson once commented, 'I don't mind people telling me how awful I am, providing they offer me a life-line to help me to be better ... but no one ever does.'

Jesus was completely different. He faced all the trials and temptations of life yet remained totally consistent in following his Father's will.

A Perfect Life

Throughout his time on earth Jesus lived in complete obedience to the will of his Father; by so doing, he initiated a totally new era on earth. Here were illustrated all those principles which God longed to bring to birth within his own people.

A new direction: Jesus took his orders from the Holy Spirit. So we read in Luke's Gospel 'Jesus ... was led by the Spirit into the desert' (Luke 4:1) to be tempted there by Satan. In leading Jesus, the Spirit did not simply direct him and then dump him; Jesus went into the desert full of the Spirit and emerged in the power of the Spirit. The Holy Spirit not only guided Jesus into God's way but equipped him to deal with each situation. By following God's directive Spirit, Jesus received all that he needed to defeat Satan's temptations and to stride ahead into his life's work.

A new authority: it took a Roman sergeant-major to recognise that a life lived in complete submission to God's direction possessed an authority which the world had never seen before. 'Just give the order, and my servant will get well. I, too, am a man placed under the authority of superior officers, and I have soldiers under me. I order this one, "Go!" and he goes' (Luke 7:7,8). It was a plain and simple fact that no one would respond to the soldier just because of his own authority. Instead, it was that delegated power which he received through the Roman military chain of command, handed down from Caesar himself, which made the difference. In the same way, when we enjoy what it means to live a life in the Spirit and therefore come under his divine direction, we can begin to know what it means to live under the authority of God himself.

A new obedience: Jesus followed only where the Spirit led him, and that is why he could confidently assert to his Father, 'I have finished the work you gave me to do' (John 17:4). Jesus did just exactly what his Father required, as the Spirit revealed it to him. In his lifetime, Jesus gave the perfect example of a life lived under the authority of and in the power of the Holy Spirit rather than by human endeavour. That is the kind of obedience required from us as well.

A Proper Division

In his letter to the Thessalonian church, Paul outlines the structure of man. He asks that God would 'keep your whole being - spirit, soul and body – free from every fault' (1 Thess 5:23). The writer of the Epistle to the Hebrews similarly speaks of the soul and the spirit (Heb 4:12).

This does not mean that men and women are made up of three separate parts that we could take apart and lay side by side on a table. Despite the way some preachers phrase it, the truth is that one rarely encounters a disembodied soul making an ethereal response to an altar call! Instead, Scripture demonstrates that our body, soul and spirit represent three different aspects of our being and that they are intimately bound together. Each fulfils a different function and together they represent our ability to respond and operate in different areas.

The body provides our contact with the outside world through the operation of the five senses: taste, smell, hearing, sight and touch. The spirit gives us our area of contact with God through communion, discerning his will and allowing his creativity to operate through us. The soul is the seat of our emotions, our intellect and our will. It is the latter that acts as a valve, determining the degree to which we are controlled by God's Spirit, as we respond to him in our spirits rather than from our selfish human desires.

Many who have no commitment to Jesus Christ at all have made the intellectual and emotional decision to try to imitate his purity, humility and love. They have tried by their own efforts, and many have made a pretty good job of it.

But God wants his people to enjoy a totally new dimension of life, not just an imitation. We are called not just to copy Jesus but actually to partake of his nature so that the Holy Spirit may radiate the glory of God through our lives. It may be hard to tell the imitation from the real thing but one is the product of human effort while the other is a divine initiative.

Tragically, many Christians fall into the same trap. We try by our hard work to do the Holy Spirit's job for him, often with pitiful results. Andrew Murray has suggested that both the church and individual Christians must dread the excessive activity of the soul. The proud mind and intrusive will of man can create the most dreadful hindrance to our proper development into spiritual maturity.

Too many of us as Christians are content with what we are. For many, to be respected by their neighbours and to live upright, kind, compassionate and orthodox Christian lives appears to them to be more than sufficient. Too often they are simply trying to find God through their own intellect, to respond to him with their own emotions and to serve him as an act of their own will. The truth is that before we can know God, respond to him or serve him, we need first to allow his

Spirit to breathe new life into our spirits. Then our minds, our emotions and our wills are driven by, motivated by and submitted to the life of the Spirit of God.

We all need to be controlled not by our own selfish desires but by the Spirit. It is not enough to determine within our souls – our mind, will and emotions – that we will follow Christ. We must allow the whole of our lives to be determined by our spirit – our capacity to receive the Holy Spirit, to love God and to live in his strength not our own. The great preacher F B Meyer is only one of the many who have affirmed that if they had not known about the dividing of spirit and soul then it would be hard to imagine what the condition of their spiritual life would have been.

A Personal Discovery

Without doubt, one of the most crushing and humiliating experiences in our Christian lives is that awful moment when we realise that we have performed actions which, judged by our standards, were good but were not in the purpose and intention of God.

Even after overcoming basic sin, our spiritual battle has only just begun. Early victories came only with the Holy Spirit's help. Our on-going struggle cannot be carried on in our own strength. 'How can you be so foolish! You began by God's Spirit; do you now want to finish by your own power?' (Gal 3:3).

We can be so well-intentioned but so dreadfully wrong. That is why Jesus repeated one instruction on so many occasions. It is also why the Holy Spirit inspired the Gospel writers to record the demand seven times in their four books that the life controlled by personal ambitions, desires, decisions and activity must die. No other verdict would be adequate. For 'those who try to gain their own life will lose it; but those who lose their life for my sake will gain it' (Matt 10:39; 16:25; Mark 8:35; Luke 9:24; 14:26; 17:33; John 12:25).

The Greek word translated 'life' here (and in most modern versions) is, more literally, 'soul'. Jesus' point is that life lived

Living by the Spirit

for personal ends in our own strength is futile - once we give up on self-centred lifestyles and concentrate on seeking to live in the power of the Spirit, then our lives will suddenly become profitable and gain eternal value.

A Precious Destiny

Jesus freely confessed that 'the Son can do nothing on his own ... I can do nothing on my own authority' (John 5:19, 30).

Never satisfied just with going about doing good, Jesus always waited for his Father's best. He waited until the Spirit moved. So he delayed eighteen years in a carpenter's workshop.

The hours Jesus spent in prayer with his Father were all to ensure that his attitude would always be, 'Not my will ... but your will be done' (Luke 22:42).

While we rush around doing this or that for the Lord, we should learn from Jesus. He waited and listened then allowed the Holy Spirit to equip and direct him. Without this kind of commitment, our self-motivated dedication will generate good things that can never amount to more than wood, grass or straw.

It is only as we place our mind, emotions and will completely at the disposal of the Holy Spirit, that our labours can have any value. Only as we first listen to the voice of the master-builder will anything of eternal worth be created.

As we place each well-intentioned activity in the hands of Jesus, we must relinquish it. We are called to act under orders. We must not accept the perverted logic of this age which assumes that once we have seen a need, we have received God's call. It is only that which God places in our hands to perform which may have any call on our time or effort. As day by day we surrender to the direction of the Holy Spirit we can rise up in confidence and begin to go about our Father's business, knowing that we are not going alone.

The Apostle Paul, having examined all his failures, assesses life in this way: 'Those who live as their human nature tells them have their minds controlled by what human nature wants. Those who live as the Spirit tells them to have their minds controlled by what the Spirit wants. To be controlled by human nature results in death: to be controlled by the Spirit results in life and peace' (Rom 8:5,6). He sees a simple answer to human failure: 'If by the Spirit you put to death your sinful actions, you will live' (Rom 8:13).

That is what leads Paul to his ultimate conclusion. He affirms that 'those who are led by God's Spirit are God's children. For the Spirit that God has given you does not make you slaves and cause you to be afraid; instead the Spirit makes you God's children' (Rom 8:14,15).

It is therefore only as he works out his purposes within our lives that we can begin to discover our destiny, to know what we were made to be - sons of God, his own children, full of confidence that he is going to use us to perform his purposes both here and for eternity.

To experience God at work in our lives in this way will involve not a one-off event but a consistent laying-down of our lives for his service. Such surrender has to be a day-by-day experience. It will not be easy but step by step, the Holy Spirit will lead us until we recognise with desperation that we are not all we should be. It is here that hope comes in because we also recognise that change is actually in progress. I have learned to appreciate the young girl who once gave me a badge on which was boldly written, 'Please have patience, God isn't finished with me yet!'

Other Resources from Scripture Union

Closer to God
Reading the Bible in the power of the Holy Spirit
ISSN 1362-914X, £2.50 per quarter.

Quarterly notes with a creative and reflective approach and emphasising renewal. There is a Bible reading with notes for every day of the week, together with 'going deeper' meditations, special features and theme weeks.

Sitting at the Feet of Jesus

Stephen and Jacalyn Eyre
ISBN 1 85999 020 7, £3.50

This Spiritual Encounter Guide on the Sermon on the Mount offers a fresh approach to personal devotion for new or long-time Christians. The aim of these Bible studies is to help readers find intimacy with God. The book contains one month's Bible reading material.

Journey into the Bible

John Drane
ISBN: 1 85999 409 1, £4.99

In his usual thought-provoking and accessible style John Drane gives a stimulating introduction to many of the issues raised by reading the Bible today. Designed especially for those who are struggling to come to terms with the Bible.

Light from a Dark Star
Where's God when my world falls apart?
Wayne Kirkland

ISBN: 1 85999 515 2, £4.99

It's the big question that won't go away. Why does God allow suffering? There are no simple answers in this book. No attempts to shrug off the serious challenges to faith which the question raises. Rather it engages compassionately with the suffereings of real people, grappling with slippery issues, in a discovery of some intriguing perspectives.

Knowing God's Ways
A user's guide to the Old Testament
Patton Taylor

ISBN: 1 85999 349 4, £6.99

Do you find the Old Testament difficult to get into? If you've been looking for some help in making sense of it all, then this book by a professor at Union Theological College in Belfast is what you've been looking for! His accessible. user-friendly approach will help you gain a clear overview of the Old Testament, understand different genres, and apply biblical teaching to today's world.

Dangerous Praying
Inspirational Ideas for individuals and groups
David Spriggs

ISBN: 1 85999335 4, £6.99

Drawing on Paul's letter to the Ephesians, this creative book challenges us to be bold when we pray, both in what we pray for and how we pray. David Spriggs presents us with 101 practical ideas and strategies to help us develop a courageous prayer life, whether in a group or individually.

Through the Bible in a Year
A spiritual journal
Dennis Lennon

ISBN 1 85999 196 3, £9.99

A new syllabus constructed around eleven themes, gives an overarching picture of the whole Bible story. There is space for the reader to keep a written record of their spiritual journey.

Ready to Grow
Practical steps to knowing God better
Alan Harkness

ISBN 0 949720 71 2, £5.99

An attractive and practical book to encourage believers to make time with God a regular part of their lives. Includes chapters on preparation, getting started, the practicalities, sharing what you have learned, and different methods of combining Bible reading and prayer.

Faith and Common Sense
Living boldly, choosing wisely
David Dewey

ISBN: 1 85999302 8, £4.99

This unusual book explores how we can live riskily yet sensibly. Drawing on the lives of key Bible characters like Peter, the author first lays a solid biblical and theological foundation for achieving a balance. Then follows a practical look at areas in our lives where a need for that balance is vital - healing, the gifts of the Spirit, work, money, failure and guidance.

The Bible Unwrapped
Developing your Bible skills
David Dewey
ISBN: 1 85999 533 0, £5.99

Is the Bible something of a closed book to you? Here you'll find help in finding your way around the Bible, and in grasping the big picture of the Bible's message. You'll also learn to appreciate the different types of literature in the Bible and be introduced to eight different approaches to Bible study. Clear and accurate charts and diagrams and a helpful glossary add value.

How to read the Bible for all its worth

Gordon Fee and Douglas Stuart
ISBN 1 86201 974 5, £7.50

This contemporary classic deals in considerable detail with the principles we need to adopt in studying different biblical genres. The authors, both professors in their respective fields of Old Testament and New Testament, explain clearly and carefully the principles underlying responsible biblical interpreatation and application to the contemporary world. There's no other book as good in its field!

Thank God it's Monday
Ministry in the Workplace
Mark Greene
ISBN: 1 85999 503 9, £4.99

Fun, fast, and full of stories, this highly practical book looks at how we can make the most of our time at work, helping us to see our jobs, our co-workers and our bosses the way God does. The third edition of this highly influential classic features an updated resource section and a new chapter on integrating life and work, helping us see how our work life, as well as our weekend life, can be lived fruitfully for God.